Crop Physiology

NEW INDIA PUBLISHING AGENCY
New Delhi-110 034

Crop Physiology
A Terminology Book

P. Boominathan
Associate Professor (Crop Physiology)
Tamilnadu Agricultural University
Coimbatore, Tamil Nadu

S. Nadaradjan
Associate Professor (Crop Physiology)
Pandit Jawaharlal Nehru College of Agriculture
(Affiliated to TNAU, Coimbatore, Tamil Nadu, India)
Karaikal, Pondicheery

A. Senthil
Associate Professor (Crop Physiology)
Tamilnadu Agricultural University
Coimbatore, Tamil Nadu

NEW INDIA PUBLISHING AGENCY
New Delhi-110 034

NEW INDIA PUBLISHING AGENCY
101, Vikas Surya Plaza, CU Block, LSC Market
Pitam Pura, New Delhi – 110 034, India
Email: info@nipabooks.com
Web: www.nipabooks.com

For customer assistance, please contact
Phone: + 91-11-27 34 17 17 Fax: + 91-11- 27 34 16 16
E-Mail: feedbacks@nipabooks.com

ISBN: 978-93-90175-16-9

Composed and Designed by NIPA.

Dedicated to
Our beloved teachers

Dr. T. G. Prasad and Dr. M. Udayakumar
Professors of Crop Physiology (Rtd)
GKVK, University of Agricultural Sciences (Bengaluru)

Preface

Plant physiology is one of the most important disciplines of biological sciences. In recent times, it has gained significant attention from scientists and students working in different area of life science. It is a science that links fundamentals and applications, there by invites many people including academicians, researchers to read and understand the various aspects of Crop physiology. Although, many textbooks available for plant physiology, difficulty in understanding the terminologies in Crop physiology become a hindrance to fully utilizing the textbooks of Crop physiology. To full fill the needs of the students and scientists working in the area of plant science, efforts were made to write this book which has come up in this form.

This book has most of the terminology which is commonly used mainly in Crop physiology and also from biochemistry, plant breeding & genetics, agronomy, soil science. Besides, few statistical terms that are commonly used in biological research also included. This book will be of immense use to the undergraduates and postgraduates' students of agriculture, biochemistry, and botany and would also helpful in various competitive exams including UPSC, TNPSC, Agricultural officers, Horticultural officers and other exams.

Suggestions for the improvement of the book from the scientists and students would always be appreciated.

Authors

Contents

A

Abiotic stress: Unfavourable situation created by non-living factors to the growth and development of plants. Factors include water, temperature, soluble salts, heavy metals, etc.

Abscissic acid (ABA): A plant hormone belongs to isoprenoid compounds. It is also known as stress hormone since it has relevance in stress tolerance in plants. Some of the physiological effects of ABA are closing of stomata, synthesis of osmolytes and seed dormancy.

Abscission layer: Distinct layer of cells with weakened cell walls in abscission zone.

Abscission zone: A region near the base of petiole of leaf which contain abscission layer.

Abscission: It is the natural processes of shedding of plant organs like leaves, flowers, and fruits. It takes place either after maturing or pre-maturing of organs. The process is characterized by the degradation of cell walls at the point where the organs attached to the plant.

Absolute Growth Rate (AGR): It is the simplest index to measure the growth rate of plant or plant organ. It is the actual growth rate occurred in plant per unit time. It gives absolute values of biomass between two intervals. It is mainly used for a single plant or single plant organ e.g. Leaf growth, plant weight etc.

AGR = $W_2 - W_1 / t_2 - t_1$ (g.day^{-1}), Where, W_1 and W_2 are the plant dry weight at t_1 and t_2 times respectively

Absolute zero: The theoretical temperature at which substances possess no thermal energy and at which all molecular activity ceases which is equal to –273.15°C.

Absorption spectrum: A graphical representation of specific absorption of light by a substance plotted against wavelength of light.

Abzyme: An antibody acting as enzyme also called as catmab means catalytic monoclonal biosynthesis.

ACC oxidase: The enzme that catalyses the oxidation of ACC to ethylene in final step of ethylene biosynthesis.

Accessory pigments: Pigments which absorb light energy and transfer to reaction centre.

Acclimatization: Acclimatization is the gradual, long-term responses of an organism to changes in its environment. If tolerance increases as a result of exposure to prior stress, the plant is said to be acclimated. Such responses are more or less habitual and reversible when environmental conditions revert to an earlier state.

Achene: A small, usually single-seeded, dry indehiscent fruit, *e.g.*, lettuce.

Acid growth: Cell wall growth in acidic pH due to extrusion of protons across plasmamembrane.

Actin: A protein found in combination of myosin in muscle also an important component of cytoskeleton of many eukaryotes.

Action spectrum: An action spectrum is the rate of a physiological activity plotted against wavelength of light. Action spectrum is the term used to describe a plot of intensity of a certain phenomenon such as rate of photosynthesis as a function of the different wavelengths of light.

Activated complex: The highest free energy state of a complex in the formation of product from reactants.

Active absorption: It is the absorption of water or minerals by roots by utilising metabolic energy (ATP) generated by the root respiration.

Active site: The region of the enzyme molecule that binds the substrate and transforms into product.

Active transport: It is the movement of ions or molecules across membrane from region of lower concentration to the region of higher concentration against concentration gradient with spending of energy.

Acylation: The introduction of an acyl group (RCO^-) into a compound.

Adaptation: It refers to a genetically determined level of resistance acquired by a process of selection over many generations.

Adequate zone: For each essential nutrient required by the plants, the specific concentration range within which its requirements are satisfied for a plant is called the adequate zone.

Adhesion: Adhesion is the tendency of attaching of dissimilar particles or surfaces to one another.

Aerobic respiration: Respiration which takes place in the presence of oxygen.

Aeroponics: It is the process of growing plants in an air or an aggregate medium.

Alcoholic fermentation: Anaerobic steps occurring after glycolysis that breakdown pyruvic acid into ethanol and carbondioxide when there is no oxygen.

Aldose: A simple sugar in which carbonyl carbon atom is an aldehyde.

Aleurone layer: Layer of aleurone cells surrounding the starchy endosperm in cereal grains. It is the source of hydrolytic enzyme that degrades starch and other polymers during germination.

Alkaloids: A group of nitrogenous secondary metabolites of plant origin especially produced by many vascular plants.

Allele: An alternate form of a gene at a specific locus.

Allelochemicals: Toxic chemicals produced by plant and released in the environment in order to defend itself against a competing plant or herbivores. These chemicals exert a detrimental physiological effect on other organism when released in the environment. These are primarily a subset of secondary metabolites.

Allelopathy: It is a biological phenomenon by which an organism/plant produces one or more bio-chemicals that has negative influence on the germination, growth, survival, and reproduction of other organisms which competes for resource.

Allocation: Flow of photoassimilates into various compartments or biochemical pathways within source and sink regions.

Allometry: Simple allometry obtains when the relative growth rates of two measured attributes of an organ or organism, *y* and *x,* are in a constant proportion.

Ameliorate: To provide a treatment or set of conditions that reduce the impact of stress by altering the time course of symptom development. Thus, amelioration is confined to describing changes in the tolerance of the plant tissue to the imposed chilling stress.

Ammonification: Conversion of organic nitrogen to ammonium ions by microbes present in the soil is called ammonification. The source of nitrogen in the organic soil are animal excreta and decaying plant which are acted upon by ammonifying saprotrophic bacteria such as *bacillus ramosus*, *bacilulus vulgaris* and *actinomycetes*.

Amphibolic pathway: During aerobic respiration the organic substrates are broken down into simple substances such as CO_2 and water. However it also produces many intermediate organic compounds which form the starting compound for the synthesis of other complex substances required for the cell. Therefore, respiration is said to be both catabolic and anabolic and is referred as amphibolic pathway.

Anaerobic respiration: Respiration which takes place in the absence of oxygen leading to lesser generation of ATP.

Anaerobic stress: A stress imposed on an organism as a result of the absence of the free oxygen of air due to flooding.

Analysis of variance: is a procedure for testing the equality of the means of two or more treatments by partitioning the variability into the amount caused by differences among the treatment means and the amount caused by differences among the experimental units within the treatments.

Anisotropic growth: Magnitude of growth vector differs in different directions

Anisotropic: Having different properties along different directions.

Annuals: A plant with a life cycle from seed to seed that is completed in only one growing season or one year.

Anthesis: The period or stage of bud opening and expansion of the flower. Sometimes specifically refers to the bursting of anthers to release pollen.

Antifreeze protiens: Antifreeze proteins (AFPs) or ice structuring proteins (ISPs) refer to a class of polypeptides produced by certain vertebrates, plants, fungi and bacteria that permit the survival of respective organism in subzero environments. AFPs bind to small ice crystals formed inside the cell due to freezing temperature to inhibit growth and recrystallization of ice inside the cell.

Anticodon: A nucleotide triplet complementary to a codon.

Antiflorigen: A transmissible stimulus that maintains the vegetative state in plant.

Antitranspirants: Substances when applied as foliar on plants, reduces transpiration whereby water loss from the plants is reduced.

Apical bud: An apical bud is the primary growing point located at the top of the plant. It is the main growth area in most plants.

Apical dominance: The dominance of apical bud in terms of suppressing the lateral bud is known as Apical dominance**.** The plant hormone responsible for the Apical dominance is Auxin. This is produced in the apical region and translocated to the sub-apical region and induce cell elongation. When the apical bud is removed, the lateral buds starts to emerge.

Apical meristem: Meristematic region (actively growing region) present on the apical portion of plant and which decides the vertical growth of plants.

Apomixis: Apomixis is the process where the seeds are produced without fertilization.

Apoplast: The interconnecting cell walls and water filled xylem elements in a plant through which water and dissolved solutes can move freely. It is the space between the cells.

Apoplastic pathway: The apoplast path of water movement includes cell wall and intercellular spaces, which are fully permeable. The water can reach up to endodermis through apoplast. It consists of non-living parts of plant body, i.e., cell walls and intercellular spaces.

Aquaporins: Aquaporins (AQP) are integral membrane proteins that serve as channels in the transfer of water, and in some cases, small solutes across the membrane. They are conserved in bacteria, plants, and animals. Structural analyses of the molecules have revealed the presence of a pore in the center of each aquaporin molecule.

Aril: Outgrowth of funiculus, raphe, or integuments; or fleshy integuments or seed coat, a sarcotesta. Arils probably often aid seed dispersal, by drawing attention to the seed after the fruit has dehisced, and by providing food as an attractant reward to the disperser. The aril of the nutmeg produces the spice mace and the seed itself is the nutmeg.

Arillate: General term for an outgrowth from the funiculus, seed coat or chalaza; or a fleshy seed coat.

ATP Phosphatase: A phosphatase is an enzyme that removes a phosphate group from its substrate by hydrolysing phosphoric acid monoesters into a phosphate ion and a molecule with a free hydroxyl group. This action is directly opposite to that of phosphorylases and kinases, which attach phosphate groups to their substrates by using energetic molecules like ATP.

ATP synthase: It is an important enzyme that is responsible for synthesis of energy storage molecule ATP.

ATP: (Adenosine tri phosphate) It is the energy source molecule for all biological activity. ATP powers energy for cell growth, cell division.

Auxin: Auxin is a plant hormone. Chemically it is a indole compound. The physiological role of auxins are apical dominance, inhibition of lateral buds, induction of rooting in cutting, prevention of fruit or flower drop, tropism etc. Indole acetic acid is the only naturally occurring auxin in plants.

Axillary meristem: Meristems in the angle (axil) formed by the leaf petiole and the stem; potentially capable of becoming branch.

B

Bacteriochlorophylls: A group of light absorbing photosynthetic green pigments of anoxygenic photosynthetic bacteria.

Ballistic transformation: The use of a particle gun to insert foreign DNA into a host.

Beneficial elements: These are the elements that help to optimize the growth and development only in some species. It is not essential to all the plants. Aluminum is beneficial to some species that are adapted to acidic soils. Cobalt can have a number of beneficial effects, especially in leguminous plants.

Betalains: Highly coloured nitrogen containing glycosylated compound in the category of alkaloids imparting red-purple and yellow colour in plants of centropsermae (*e.g.*, beet root).

Beta-oxidation: Breakdown of fatty acids into Acetyl co-A by successive oxidation. It is the first step of lipids breakdown.

Bidirectional transport: Simultaneous transport of solutes in opposite directions in the same file of sieve elements. Bidirectional transport may occur under some circumstances. For *e.g.*, in a file of cell, as a result of cytoplasmic streaming.

Biennial: A plant that lives two growing seasons and flowers and dies during the second season. Typically, biennials grow vegetatively during the first season and flowers and die in the second season.

Biochemistry: Biochemistry deals with the structures, functions and interactions of biological macromolecules, such as proteins, nucleic acids, carbohydrates and lipids, which provide the structure of cells and perform many of the functions associated with life.

Bioinformatics: It is collection, storage and analysis of DNA and protein sequence by computerized systems.

Biological clock: An innate mechanism that controls the physiological activities of an organism which change on a daily, seasonal, yearly or other regular cycle. Time measuring systems in plants which is based on endogenous circadian rhythms.

Biological cycle: Sequence of events in an organism that repeat in the same order and at the same interval through time.

Biological life cycle: Biological life cycle is the sequence of life stages that an organism undergoes from birth to reproduction ending with the generation of the offspring.

Biological membrane: It is semipermable membrane. It has lipid bilayer interspersed with proteins. It has intrinsic and extrinsic proteins. It plays an important role in transport of ions in and out of cytoplasm.

Biological nitrogen fixation: Living organisms like bacteria converting atmospheric nitrogen into ammonia either by symbiotic relationship with host or free living organism.

Biosalinity: Interplay of saline habitats and the organisms living within them.

Biotic stress: Stress created by living organisms like insects, pathogens or weeds to plants.

Biotin: A vitamin that act as coenzyme in carboxylation reactions.

Blue light responses: Photomorphogenetic responses of plants to blue light mediated through cryptochrome such as phototropism, stomatal opening and sun tracking of leaves.

Bolting: is the production of a flowering stem (or stems) on agricultural and horticultural crops before the crop is harvested, in a natural attempt to produce seeds and reproduce.

Bound water : The quantity of water in a tissue that is strongly held by adsorptive (matric) forces and is difficult to remove by tissue drying.

Brassinolide: A very common and biologically active brassinosteriods in plants.

Brassinosteriod: Brassinosteroids are a class of polyhydroxy steroids that have been recognized as a sixth class of plant hormones. These were first explored nearly 40 years ago, scientists reported that promotion in stem elongation and cell division by the treatment of organic extracts of rapeseed (*Brassica napus*) pollen.

Bronzing: Brownish leaf discolouration in plants is called bronzing due to deficiency of essential elements. In Legumes, bronzing caused by deficiency micro nutrient like chlorine.

Brownian movements: Continuous and rapid zig-zag motion of the suspended particles in a colloidal solution resulting from unequal bombardment of the particles of dispersed phase by molecules of dispersion medium.

Bud dormancy: During the developmental cycle of the plant, at some phase or the other certain structure like buds, go through a period of temporary suspension of growth activity. Such a state is called bud dormancy.

Buffer action: The ability of the buffer solution to resist the changes in pH value on the addition of small amount of an acid or a base is known as buffer action.

Buffer: A buffer solution is an aqueous solution consisting of a mixture of a weak acid and its conjugate base, or vice versa. Its pH changes very little when a small amount of strong acid or base is added to it.

C

C_3 cycle or Calvin cycle: It is a process of dark reaction of photosynthesis. It is also called as photosynthetic carbon reduction cycle which results in the production of sugars. It occurs not only in C_3 plants but also in C_4 and CAM pathway also. It occurs in the mesophyll cells. It is described in three stages: (1) Carboxylation, (2) Reduction, (3) Regeneration.

C_3 plants: Group of plants with calvin cycle wherein the first stable product is 3-phosphoglyceric acid, a three carbon compound. *e.g.*, rice, wheat, barley.

C_4 cycle: C_4 cycle may also referred to as the dicarboxylic acid cycle or Hatch and Slack Cycle. The first stable product is a C_4 compounds like oxaloacetic acid. Here CO_2 molecule is accepted by phosphoenol pyruvate in the carboxylation reaction. The main purpose of this cycle is carbondioxide enrichment.

C_4 plants: Plants with Hatch-slack pathway and kranz anatomy of leaves in which the first stable product is four carbon compound, oxaloacetic acid. These plants posses high photosynthetic efficiency and low photorespiration rate. *e.g.*, sugarcane, maize, sorghum.

Calcium carbide: Calcium carbide is a chemical compound with the chemical formula of $CaCr_2$. It is mainly used in ripening fruits in large scale, eventhough it is not advised to use this chemicals as it contains traces of arsenic and phosphorus, which is harmful to consumers. Calcium carbide when it comes in contact with moisture in atmosphere produces acetylene, which has a similar properties like ethylene, which is known as ripening hormone.

Callose: A carbohydrate, with β $(1\rightarrow3)$ glucan synthesized in sieve elements of phloem.

Callus: Mass of undifferentiated cells and unorganized growth of cells.

Calmodulin: A calcium binding protein that is involved in many calcium driven metabolic reactions in eukaryotic cells. This protein is activated by binding of calcium.

CAM plants: Plants in which crassulacean acid metabolism (CAM) occurs wherein atmospheric CO_2 is taken during night time through stomata and fixed as malate and stored in vacuole. During day time, decarboxylation of malate releases CO_2 which is taken for calvin cycle and assimilated.

Capillary Force Theory: Given by Boehm. According to this theory, xylem vessels act as minute capillaries and water rises in these capillaries due to capillary action.

Carbondioxide: Carbondioxide is a colourless and odourless gas. This naturally occuring chemical compound is composed of carbon atom and covalently double bonded to two oxygen atoms. Diffusion of this CO_2 into plant leads to a physiological process called photosynthesis.

Carbonidioxide compensation point: Concentration of CO_2 at which CO_2 taken for photosynthesis equal CO_2 released in respiration.

Carboxylation: It is the process of addition of CO_2 to any molecule. Usually mediated by Carboxylase enzyme. In calvin cycle, Carboxylation is the fixation of CO_2 into a stable organic intermediate.

Carboxysomes: Carboxysomes are bacterial organelles consisting of polyhedral protein shells filled with the enzyme Ribulose-1,5-bisphosphate carboxylase/ oxygenase (RuBisCO) -the predominant enzyme in carbon fixation and the rate limiting enzyme in the Calvin Cycle-and a carbonic anhydrase.

Caruncle: A reduced aril, in the form of a fleshy, often waxy or oily, outgrowth near the hilum of some seeds. Usually it is brightly colored. It acts as an aid to dispersal. Viola seeds have an oily caruncle and are sought and dispersed by ants.

Caruncułate: Seed with an excrescent outgrowth from integuments near the hilum, as in Euphorbia.

Caryopsis: A dry, nut-like fruit typical of grasses, *e.g.*, a cereal grain. It is an achene with the ovary wall united with the seed coat.

Casparian strip: A band or strip of hydrophobic substance suberin running completely round radial and transverse walls of endodermal cells, named after R. Caspary.

Catabolism: A metabolic process in which complex molecules are broken down into simple ones with the release of energy; destructive metabolism. It is the set of metabolic pathways that breaks down molecules into smaller units that are either oxidized to release energy or used in other anabolic reactions.

Cation exchange capacity (CEC): The total quantity of cations that a soil or other material can adsorb at a specific pH, usually expressed as centimoles of a specific cation per kilogram of exchanger.

Caulogenesis: The development of shoot from the callus is called caulogenesis.

Cavitation: Spontaneous occurrence of a vapor phase in a liquid under tension. It occurs in the xylem of plant under moderate to severe water stress resulting in a reduced capacity of the xylem to conduct water.

Cell cycle: The cell cycle or cell-division cycle is the series of events that take place in a cell leading to its division and duplication of its DNA (DNA replication) to produce two daughter cells.

Cell Differentiation: Cell differentiation refers to a situation in which meristematic cells while growing give rise to 2 or more types of cells which are qualitatively different from one another.

Cell division: Cell division is a very important process in all living organisms. During the division of a cell, DNA replication and cell growth also take place. All these processes, cell division, DNA replication, and cell growth, hence, have to take place in a coordinated way to ensure correct division and formation of progeny cells containing intact genomes.

Cell elongation: Cell elongation is a developmental process that is regulated by light and phytohormones and is of critical importance for plant growth.

Cell Enlargement: During this phase, the newly formed cells absorb water by osmosis resulting in the increased turgidity and expansion and dialation of the elastic cell wall. In the initial stages, the cell enlargement occurs in all directions but is later confined to a specific direction.

Cell Formation: During this phase, the meristematic cells divide to form new cells. Division is restricted to the apical meristems, both at root and shoot tips. The newly formed daughter cells are thin walled and have dense protoplasm. The daughter cells have the same number of chromosomes and the same genetic constitution.

Cell theory: The cell is structural and functional unit of all plants and animals and new cells arise from division of preexisting cells.

Cell wall: Outer protective coating around the protoplast in most plants including fungi and bacteria that is made up of chiefly carbohydrates.

Cell: It is the basic unit of living organisms. The smallest structural and functional unit of an organism, which is typically microscopic and consists of cytoplasm and a nucleus enclosed in a membrane.

Cellular respiration: It is the set of metabolic reactions and processes that take place in the cells of organisms to convert biochemical compounds into ATP and then release waste products.

Cellulose: Long straight chain polysaccharide consisting of large number of $\beta(1\rightarrow4)$ linked D-glucopyranose units. It is most abundant cell wall polysaccharide of plants and organic substance on earth.

Chalaza: Non-micropylar end of the seed. The base of an ovule bearing an embryo sac surrounded by integuments.

Chaperons: Proteins that facilitate proper folding of other proteins and also assembly of multiple polypeptides into larger structure. They are functionally related groups of proteins. These proteins assist covalent folding.

Chemical messenger: A Chemical messenger is any compound that serves to transmit the message. A chemical messenger may refer to hormone, neurotransmitter, neuropeptide and pheromone.

Chemiosmotic production of ATP: Chemiosmosis is the movement of ions across a selectively permeable membrane, down their electrochemical gradient. More specifically, it relates to the generation of ATP by the movement of hydrogen ions across a membrane during cellular respiration or photosynthesis. Hydrogen ions will diffuse from an area of high proton concentration to an area of lower concentration, and an electrochemical concentration gradient of protons across a membrane can be harnessed to make ATP.

Chemoautotroph: An organism that derives its carbon from inorganic carbon source while the energy is obtained from oxidation of chemical substances.

Chemotropism: It is the plant movement in response to a chemical substance. It is also the growth of organisms such as bacteria and plants, navigated by chemical stimulus from the outside of the organism or organism part. The response of the organism or organism part is termed 'positive' if the growth is towards the stimulus or 'negative' if the growth is away from the stimulus. An example of chemo-tropic movement can be seen during the growth of the pollen tube, where growth is always towards the ovules.

Chilling injury: A descriptive term for the physiological injury to many plants, particularly those warm-season species (e.g., crops) of tropical or sub-tropical origin, when they are exposed to low, but non-freezing temperatures.

Chilling temperature: Any temperature below the critical temperature, but above freezing, that causes injury.

Chilling tolerance: The ability of chilling-sensitive plants or plant parts, to endure the metabolic dysfunction that result from exposure to chilling temperatures and to survive when the stress is not sustained beyond a certain lethal point. Chilling tolerance is used to describe this differential response to chilling stress and should be confined to describing differences in the time and course of the development of chilling injury symptoms.

Chilling: The act of exposing plant material to a non-freezing low temperature. This exposure may or may not be beneficial to the plant.

Chilling-insensitive: Those plants that typically continue to grow and develop, albeit slowly, and can complete their life cycle when continuously exposed to chilling temperatures. These plants are primarily cool season species of temperate.

Chilling-sensitive plants: Those plants that are injured by exposure to temperatures below about 10 °C to 15 °C, but above freezing. All stages of growth and development of the entire plant (except perhaps the dry seed) are susceptible. However, these temperatures do not limit growth or geographic distribution of these species as exhibited

Chitin: A mucopolysaccharide, chief component of fungal cell walls and found abundant in Arthropods.

Chlorophylls: A group of light absorbing green photosynthetic pigments made up of magnesium-porphyrin complexes, found in all photosynthesizing cells including bacteria.

Chloroplasts: Chloroplast is an organelle present inside Plant cell. It is the photosynthetic apparatus present in the mesophyll cells of the leaves of higher green plants. They may be discoid or ellipsiodal. It is bounded by two membranes. It has its own genome. Hence it is semiautonomous in nature.

Chlorosis: Chlorosis is a condition in which leaf produce insufficient chlorophyll and hence the leaf show yellowing symptoms.

Cholondny-went hypothesis: A classical theory proposed to explain tropism in plants states that unilateral illumination causes lateral distribution of endogenous auxin near stem apex. More auxin on the shaded side of the stem tip stimulates cells on that side to elongate more resulting in phototropic curvature.

Cholorophyll stability index (CSI): CSI is an indication of stress tolerance capacity of plants. Higher CSI values helps to withstand stress through better availability of chlorophyll. It is ratio of chlorophyll content in stressed to normal plant expressed in percentage.

Chromatin: The material of chromosomes, consisting of DNA and histone proteins.

Chromophore: Chromophore is the part of a molecule responsible for its color. The color arises when a molecule absorbs certain wavelengths of visible light and transmits or reflects others. The chromophore is a region in the molecule where the energy difference between two different molecular orbitals falls within the range of the visible spectrum. Visible light that hits the chromophore can thus be absorbed by exciting an electron from its ground state into an excited state.

Chromoplast: It is a coloured plastid other than a chloroplast, typically containing a yellow or orange pigment.

Chromosome: A Self replication module of a gene consisting of DNA and proteins. Nuclear chromosomes are physically very different from chomosomes of organelles and prokaryotes. Viral chromosoes may be DNA or RNA.

Circadian rhythm: A biological rhythm with periodicity of about 24 hours and not exactly 24 hours.

Citric acid cycle: This cycle is a part of aerobic respiration of glucose. Pyruvic acid enters this cycle and produces various intermediates. One of the intermediates is citric acid and hence this cycle is called as citric acid cycle. It is also called as Krebs cycle.

Climateric fruits: Fruits which shows sudden rise in ethylene and carbondioxide during fruit ripening.

Coding sequence: A set of codons that encode a protein codon A three-nucleotide segment of RNA specifying an amino acid or translational stop signal.

Codon: It is a three nucleotide segment of RNA specifying an aminoacid.

Co-enzyme: An organic molecule required for the activity of certain enzmes. Many vitamin play this role in enzyme functioning.

Co-factor: A Co-enzyme or an inorganic ion required for enzymatic reaction.

Cohesion: Mutual force of attraction between similar molecules. During ascent of sap, cohesion between water molecules due to hydrogen bondings provides the force that holds up column of water in the xylem.

Colchicine: An alkaloid which blocks cell division by inhibiting spindle fibres formation. This is used for production of double haploid lines.

Coleoptile: This is protective covering around plumule during germination in grass seeds. It grows as a tubular covering around the long narrow primary leaf of the seedling.

Coleorhiza: A protective sheath surrounding radical which is formed during germination of grass seeds.

Colloids: A homogeneous non-crystalline substance consisting of large molecules or ultramicroscopic particles of one substance dispersed through a second substance. Colloids include gels, sols, and emulsions; the particles do not settle, and cannot be separated out by ordinary filtering or centrifuging like those in a suspension.

Colony hybridization: A method for detecting the presence of a specific sequence of DNA among bacterial colonies on a plate.

Colony: A group of cells, normally on a plate, derived from a single cell.

Companion cells: Small parenchyma cells with dense cytoplasm and prominent nucleus, lying side by side with sieve tube cells in phloem and connected with each other through large plasmodesmata.

Compartmentalization: It is a mechanism in which excess sodium, which is toxic, stored in vacuole, so that sodium does not disturb the metabolism of the plant.

Compatibility: The coexistence of two genetic systems in the same cell or organism; *e.g., phage* with a host bacterium or organelles with a nucleus.

Compatible solutes: Organic compounds synthesized in plant cell to reduce the water potential of cell, so that to regulate the osmotic process so that water enter into plant cell. Sudden increase in this specific compound should not interfere any of the normal metabolic reactions happening in the cell. It should be compatible and hence it is called as compatible solutes. The other names are osmolytes, osmoregulants. Examples, proline, glycine betaine, sugar alcohols, sucrose. Besides, inorganic K^+ ions acts as compatible solutes.

Competitive inhibition: An inhibitor which competes with substrate for binding site of the enzyme. This inhibition is reversible and can be reversed of removal of inhibitor or by increasing substrate concentration.

Concentration: It is the ratio of solute to the total volume of solution.

Conformation: Spatial arrangements of substituent groups which are free to occupy different positions in space without breaking of any bond due to freedom of bond rotation.

Convection: The mass movement of heated liquid or gas. When used in discussions of cold hardiness, the term generally refers to mass movement of heated air.

Co-transport: This is simultaneous transport of two solutes by a single transporter across the membrane.

Cristae: A mitochondrion has two membranes, an outer and an inner, the latter deeply creased and folded thereby increasing its surface area on which the specialized reactions occur. The folds of the mitochondrion are called cristae.

Critical day length: It is the day length required by the plants to flower.

Cryo preservation: Cryopreservation or cryoconservation is a process where cells, whole tissues, or any other substances susceptible to damage caused by chemical reactivity or time are preserved by cooling to sub-zero temperatures. At low enough temperatures, any enzymatic or chemical activity which might cause damage to the material in question is effectively stopped. Cryopreservation methods seek to reach low temperatures without causing additional damage caused by the formation of ice during freezing.

Cryptochromes: Cryptochrome is a type of sensory pigment which is involved in photomorphogenesis of plants. These are a class of flavoproteins that are sensitive to blue light. They are found in plants and animals. Cryptochromes are involved in the circadian rhythms of plants and animals, and in the sensing of magnetic fields in a number of species. Cryptochrome has role in phototropism, stomatal opening and synthesis of carotenoids.

Cuticle: A plant cuticle is a protecting film, covering the epidermis of leaves, young shoots and other aerial plant organs without periderm. It consists of lipid and hydrocarbon polymers impregnated with wax and are synthesized exclusively by the epidermal cells.

Cuticular transpiration: The loss of water in the form of water vapour through the cuticle is known as cuticular transpiration. It constitutes around 5-10% of water loss.

Cyanide resistant respiration: This pathway is due to resistance of alternate oxidase to cyanide leading to continued terminal oxidation of reduced coenzymes. The electron transport from ubiquinol to O_2 *via* alternate oxidase is uncoupled with ATP synthesis.

Cyanobacteria: Blue green algae which lacks nucleus similar to bacteria belongs to prokaryotes.

Cyanogenic glucosides: A group of nitrogenous secondary metabolites in some plants releasing poisonous hydrogen cyanide (HCN) when the plants containing them are crushed. This is used as feeding deterrents to insects and herbivores.

Cyclic electron transport: Electron transport chain in chloroplast wherein electrons originate from photosystem I return back to PSII leading to synthesis of ATP without production of NADPH.

Cyclic photophosphorylation: It is a type of light reaction. Cyclic Photophosphorylation is defined as the process of production of only ATP. This process of electron transport involves only Photosystem 1 occurs in stoma lamellae. It lacks Photosystem 2 and NADP reductase enzyme. The excited electron does not pass to $NADP^+$ but it is cycled back to the PSI complex through electron transport chain.

Cycloheximide: An antibiotic which inhibits protein synthesis by blocking the peptidyl transferase of eukayotic ribosomes

Cycocel : CCC (2-chloroethyl trimethyl ammonium chloride). This is a gibberellin inhibitors that reduces the height and increases the reproductive growth leads to increase in yield.

Cytochrome b_6f: The cytochrome b_6f complex occupies a central position in the sequence of photosynthetic electron transport carriers, oxidizing plastoquinol (PQH_2) and providing the electron transfer connection between the two reaction center complexes, PS II and PS I. Cytochrome f, cytochrome b and the Rieske-type are the three component of cytochrome b_6f complex.

Cytochrome: Cytochromes are iron containing hemeproteins that are primarily responsible for the generation of ATP via electron transport. They are found either as monomeric proteins (e.g., cytochrome c) or as subunits of larger enzymatic complexes that catalyze redox reactions.

Cytokinin: It is type of plant hormone, which stimulates cell division. It is chemically substituted adenine compounds. The precursor for cytokinin is Mevolanate. Extensively used in tissue culture for callus differentiation. It promotes caulogenesis. It has role in retarding senescence, inducing lateral branches and activating certain enzymes.

Cytoplasm: Cytoplasm is the material within a living cell, excluding the cell nucleus. It comprises cytosol (the gel-like substance enclosed within the cell membrane) and the organelles. All of the contents of the cells of prokaryote organisms are contained within the cytoplasm. The cytoplasm contains 80% water and usually colorless.

Cytoplasmic streaming: Movement of cytoplasm within the cell as the result of actin-myosin interaction; different types are distinguished according to the regularity of velocity in time and space with which the cell organelles are displaced.

Cytoskeleton: It is the interconnecting network of protein filaments spread throughout the cytoplasm of Eukaryotes and responsible for controlling cell shape and assist in mobility of cell organelles or whole cells. It play important role in cell division, wall deposition and cell differentiation.

Cytosol: Cytosol is the aqueous component of the cytoplasm of a cell, within which various organelles and particles are suspended.

D

Dark reactions: It is light independent reactions occurs during daytime. This includes C_3, C_4 and CAM pathway involving the utilization of NADPH and ATP to fix CO_2 into carbohydrates. It is also called as stromal reactions.

Day neutral plants: The plants that flowers regardless of the length of the period of the light that is exposed to. They are called as day neutral plants.

DCMU (Dichlorophenyl dimethyl urea or diuron)**:** An herbicide that inhibits non-cyclic photophosophorylation specifically blocks the electron flow at the quinone acceptors of PSII, by competing for the binding site of plastoquinone that is normally occupied by PQB.

DCPIP (Dichlorophenol indophenols): A dye often used as artificial hydrogen acceptor to demonstrate in Hills reaction in isolated chloroplast in laboratory. The oxidized form is blue in alkali and red in acid, while reduced form is colourless.

Deamination: It is the enzymatic removal of amino group in the amino acid to its corresponding ketoacid.

Dedifferentiation: The living differentiated cells that have lost their capacity to divide can regain the capacity of division under certain conditions is called dedifferentiation. The development of interfascicular cambium and cork cambium from fully differentiated parenchyma cells is an example of dedifferentiation.

Deep supercooling: Ability of organisms to supercool at a temperature below that of intracellular freezing of water as low as the homogeneous nucleation point of pure water, approximately –40 °C. This mechanism to avoid freezing exists in tissue such as xylem ray parenchyma and dormant flower buds.

De-etiolation: In absence or less amount of light, the growth of seedling becomes pale yellow and tall which is reversal of etiolation.

Deficiency symptoms: A symptom caused in plants because of lack of essential nutrients which is necessary for normal growth and development.

Degree growth stage model (°GS Model): Numerical system for quantifying the annual physiological growth stages of buds of temperate plants.

Dehardening: Synonymous with deacclimation. This is reversal of hardening process leading to loss in plant tissues and organs for resistance to various stresses.

Dehydration avoidance: Ability to prevent reductions in plant water potential despite reductions in environmental water availability.

Dehydration tolerance: Ability to continue a plant function, despite reductions in plant water potential inside the cell.

DELLA-proteins: Transcriptions factors which function as repressors in GA signalling. This protein has conserved amino terminal sequence known as DELLA which denotes single letter code of amino acids.

Denaturation: Partial or complete disruption of native folded structure of protein or nucleic acid due to heat or change in pH.

Denitrification: Denitrification is a microbial facilitated process of nitrate reduction (performed by a large group of heterotrophic facultative anaerobic bacteria) that may ultimately produce molecular nitrogen (N_2) through a series of intermediate gaseous nitrogen oxide products.

Density gradient centrifugation: It is a method of centrifugation which separates cell organelles or other substances based on density in a gradient varying in solute concentration.

Desalination: The removal of salt from soil or water by physical or chemical means.

Determinate growth: Plant growth in which the main stem ends in an inflorescence or other reproductive structure and stops continuing to elongate indefinitely with only branches from the main stem having further and similarly restricted growth.

Development: Growth and differentiation over time leads to the formation of an organism with metabolic and structural complexity refers to development. The term development is used to refer the activities resulting from growth and differentiation. Development includes all changes that an organism (plant) goes through during its life cycle from germination of the seed to senescence.

Devernalization: It is the process of exposing previously vernalised seeds or plants to high temperature causing a reversion to the original non-flowering condition.

Differential thermal analysis (DTA): Method of determining the exothermic temperature difference between a reference and a sample, usually biological, being frozen, or the differential endothermic temperature of a sample being thawed.

Diffuse pressure: It describes the potential ability of a gas, liquid or solid to spread away (to diffuse) from an area of its higher concentration to an area of its lesser concentration. The net movement of molecules due to the development of a pressure which may be defined as diffusion pressure.

Diffusion pressure deficit: This term was given by Meyer. Every liquid is having a definite diffusion pressure and the diffusion pressure of pure solvent is always more than diffusion pressure of its solutions. e.g., if sugar solution is made in water. Then D.P of solutions is lower (solvent). The amount by which D.P of solutions lower than that of its pure solvent, is called diffusion pressure deficit. In case of D.P.D., the solution will try to wipe off this difference in D.P. by sucking more water (solvent) molecules and hence D.P.D.is the measure or index of sucking power and hence it is also called suction pressure (S.P) so D.P.D = S.P.

Diffusion: Diffusion is the random kinetic movement of molecules or atoms from a region of high concentration (or high chemical potential) to a region of low concentration (or low chemical potential) until the equilibrium is reached. This is also referred to as the movement of a substance down a concentration gradient. The word diffusion is derived from the Latin word, "diffundere", which means "to spread out" (if a substance is "spreading out", it is moving from an area of high concentration to an area of low concentration).

Diffusivity: The "speed" at which changes in water potential propagate within tissues and incorporates cell and wall conductances to water and their storage capacities.

Dilution: It is the action of making a more concentrated solution into less concentrated solution.

Diterpene: A terpene with 20 carbon compound with four isoprene units.

Dormancy: An inactive period in the life of an organism during which growth completely ceases ever under favourable conditions.

Drought avoidance: The ability of plants to bear periods of drought by maintaining a high plant status by saving water or getting more water is called as drought avoidance.

Drought escape: The ability of plant to complete its life cycle before soil and plant water deficits develops. Developmental plasticity and rapid phenological developments are the mechanisms under drought escape.

Drought resistance: The ability of a plant to survive or yield under drought conditions relative to other plants in the same environment. Drought tolerance, avoidance, and escape are types of drought resistance.

Drought tolerance: The ability of plants to maintain the cell metabolic activity even under low water potential is drought tolerance.

Drought: A condition in which the availability of soil water on micro and macro environmental scale is generally insufficient to supply the maximal requirements of well adapted plants.

Dry Matter Efficiency (DME): It is defined as the percent of dry matter accumulated in the grain from the total dry matter produced over the crop growth period.

E

Ectodormancy: A kind of dormancy which is due to environmental factors.

EDTA: An important chelating agent often used in modern nutrient solutions. It forms soluble complexes with metal ions such as that of iron and prevents from precipitation in the solution.

Elaiosomes: Greek élaion means "oil" and sóma means "body" , are fleshy structures that are attached to the seeds of many plant species. The elaiosome is rich in lipids and proteins, and may be variously shaped. Many plants have elaiosomes that attract ants, which take the seed to their nest and feed the elaiosome to their larvae and by which the seed get dispersed.

Electrical conductivity: Electrical conductivity is the measure of a material's ability to allow the transport of an electric charge. It is used to measure the level of salinity in water or soil. When electrical conductivity is more, then salinity is more since as salt concentration is more in water or soil, then those salts will conduct more of electricity. Normally measured in μS/cm.

Electrical impedance: The application of alternating electrical current to pre-frozen or frozen plant tissues to predict damage or measure injury, respectively.

Electrochemical gradient: An electrochemical gradient is a gradient of electrochemical potential, usually for an ion that can move across a membrane. The gradient consists of two parts, the electrical potential and a difference in the chemical concentration across a membrane. The sum of gradients of concentration and electric charge of an ion across membrane.

Electrochemical potential: The energy required to maintain separation of charge and of concentration across the membrane.

Electrochemical proton gradient: The concentration differences in protons across the membrane due to transfer of protons.

Electrolyte leakage: A technique used to determine cell or tissue viability by estimating membrane integrity.

Electron spin resonance (ESR): A spectroscopic method of locating unpaired electrons within the molecules of a paramagnetic substance.

Electron transport chain in mitochondria: It is process of oxidation of NADH and FADH2 through series of protein complexes from complex I to complex V through mobile electron carrier UQ and cytochrome c and finally to O_2 producing large amount of ATP.

Electrophoresis: The movement of a mixture of macromolecules into a semi-solid, porous medium in response to an electric field to determine its mass/charge ratio (size) or to separate it from other components. This technique is used to separate both proteins and nucleic acids.

Electrotropism: Movement of curvature in response to electrical current. Electropism is a kind of tropism which results in growth or migration of an organism, usually a cell, in response to an exogenous electric field. Electropism is known to play a role in the control of growth in cells and the development of tissues.

Embolism: The process by which xylem vessel is blocked by introduction of air bubble.

Embryo: A seed plant embryo is part of a seed, consisting of precursor tissues for the leaves, stem (hypocotyl), and root (radicle), as well as one or more cotyledons. Once the embryo begins to germinate and grow out from the seed, it is called a seedling (plantlet). Embryo is an young sporophyte, dipoid (2n), resulted due to fertilization.

Embryogenesis: Formation of embryos (*i.e.*, bipolar structure having shoot, root) from the callus called embryogenesis.

Emerson Enhancement effect: Enhancement of quantum yield by combing two beams of red and far-red light as compared to effect of beams when used separately. As a result of these experiments two photo systems were identified.

EMP pathway (Embden-Myerhof-Paranas): This first pathway in respiration takes place in cytoplasm wherein glucose is oxidized to two molecules of pyruvic acid. Under aerobic condition, pyruvic acid is converted into acetyl coA and entered into TCA cycle, while under anaerobic condition, pyruvic acid is converted into lactic acid or ethanol.

Enantiomers: Stereoisomers that are mirror image of each other. *e.g.*, D-glucose is a enantiomer of L-glucose.

Endergonic reaction: A chemical reaction which consumes energy that is with a positive free energy change.

Endogenous dormancy: Endogenous dormancy is caused by conditions within the embryo itself, and it is also often broken down into three subgroups: physiological dormancy, morphological dormancy and combined dormancy.

Endogenous rhythm: A rhythm that is not dependent on environmental parameters such as temperature, light though it may be synchronized with them.

Endoplasmic reticulum (ER): A system of double membrane throughout cytoplasm of eukaryotic cells. When it is associated with ribosome, it is rough ER, without ribosome, it is smooth ER.

Endosperm: Endosperm is a tissue produced inside the seeds of most of the flowering plants following fertilization. It surrounds the embryo and provides nutrition in the form of starch, though it can also contain oils and protein.

Endospermic seeds: Endospermic seeds are those that have an endosperm in the mature seed. It is fleshy, oily, surrounds the embryo, and functions as the sole food storage organ. Inside the seed coat, a thin and papery cotyledon is present. Monocot plants have endospermic seeds.

Endothermic reaction: A chemical reaction that consumes heat for which ΔH is positive.

Endotherms: Heat consumed during a thawing event.

Energy budget: An energy budget is a balance sheet of energy income against expenditure in plants.

Energy synthesis phase: The production of ATP, NADH cycles in glycolysis for production of products called energy synthesis phase.

Energy utilizing phase: The ATP, NADH are utilized in glycolysis for regeneration of further cycle is called as energy utilizing phase.

Energy: Energy is the property that must be transferred to an object in order to perform work – or to heat the object, and can be converted in form, but not created or destroyed. The SI unit of energy is the Joule.

Enthalpy (H): The heat content of the system.

Entner-Doudoroff pathway: An alternate pathway for the oxidation of glucose to form pyruvate other than glycolysis in few micro organisms.

Entropy (S): A thermodynamic measure of the randomness or disorder in a system.

Epicotyl: Epicotyl is the region of an embryo or seedling stem above the cotyledon. The shoot apex of the embryo which develops into the stem. In germinated seeds or seedlings referring to the portion of the stem between the cotyledons and the first leaves. Plumule is the embryonic shoot derived from the epicotyl. In dicotyledons situated between the cotyledons.

Epigeal germination: Epigeal germination is a botanical term indicating that the germination of a plant takes place above the ground. An example of a plant with epigeal germination is the common bean (*Phaseolus vulgaris*). Epigeal germination implies that the cotyledons are pushed above ground. The hypocotyl elongates while the epicotyl stays the same length. In this way, the hypocotyl pushes the cotyledon upward.

Epimers: Two stereoisomers with more than one chiral centre which differ in configuration ony at one of their centres. e.g., xylulose and ribulose, D-glucose and D-galactose

Epinasty: Downward bending of leaves is called as epinasty. Ethylene has a role in epinasty. The uneven expansion of leaves on both sides leads to downward bending of leaves.

Essential elements: Any chemical element required by an organism for healthy growth. It may be required in large amount (micro-nutrients) or in very small amounts (trace element).

Ethylene: Ethylene is a type of plant hormone. It is a gaseous hormone. It is synthesized from Methionine. It has a role in ripening of fruits, epinasty, triple response, sex expression, latex flow and senescence. It is mainly used for ripening of fruits and hence it is called as ripening hormone.

Etiolation: In absence of light, seedling becomes pale yellow, tall and slender in appearance due to lack of photomorphogenesis.

Etioplast: An organelle that develops from chloroplast or proplastid in absence of light. When exposed to light, etioplast is converted into chloroplast.

Euhalophytes: Plants which can grow at extreme salinity conditions are called as euhalophytes. A plant whose growth is maximum at a soil water salinity of about 20 dS/m.

Eukaryotes: An organism with membrane bound nucleus in the cell which might have evolved from prokaryotes that has nucleus without membrane.

Evaporation: Loss of water in form of water vapour from non-living things such as soil.

Evaporative cooling: Cooling caused by the vaporization of a liquid. In the event of cold hardiness, it would be the reduction in temperature of biological matter due to the loss of water to the atmosphere.

Evapotranspiration: It is loss of water both due to transpiration and evaporation. It is the total water use for plants. Evapotranspiration = Transpiration + Evaporation.

Excited state: The state of molecules in which the electron moved to outer orbits of radiant energy. e.g., The excitation energy in case of chlorophyll can be dissipated by resonance transfer and heat.

Exclusion: It is an adaptive mechanism adopted by plants to grow under salinity. By exclusion unwanted sodium is excluded out of plant and takes essential potassium at root and shoot.

Excretion: It is one of adaptive mechanism adopted by plants to grow under salinity. Here the plants excrete or send out the excess salt via specialized glands called as salt glands.

Exergonic: It is a metabolic or chemical process accompanied by release of energy.

Exogenous dormancy: Exogenous dormancy is caused by conditions outside the embryo and is often broken down into three subgroups. They are physical, mechanical and chemical.

Exotherm: Heat lost during a freezing event. This reaction releases energy into environment.

Expressed sequence tag (EST): cDNAs for protein genes that are expressed under selected conditions. EST often refers to a partial sequence of the cDNA used to identify sites in the genome that encode a specific gene product.

Extracellular matrix: The complex of carbohydrates and protein which forms cell walls and other structures external to the plasma membrane.

F

Facilitated diffusion: Facilitated diffusion is a movement in the direction of a concentration gradient; but it involves moving through a channel protein or a carrier protein. A channel protein is merely a pore in the membrane, and is often gated to control movement. A carrier protein has a binding site where the substance attaches and moved through the membrane.

Facultative CAM: Plants which behave as C_3 under conditions of normal water supply. However, switch over to CAM mode under conditions of water deficit.

FAD (Flavin adenine dinucleotide): A riboflavin containing co-enzyme of some oxidation reduction reactions.

Facultative long day plant: Facultative photoperiodic plants are more likely to flower under appropriate light conditions, but will eventually flower regardless of length of night.

FADH: In biochemistry, flavin adenine dinucleotide (FAD) is a redox cofactor, more specifically a prosthetic group, involved in several important reactions in metabolism. FAD can exist in three different redox states, which are quinone, semiquinone and hydroquinone. FAD is converted between these states by accepting or donating electrons. FAD, in its full oxidised form or quinone form, accepts two electrons and two protons to become $FADH_2$ (hydroquinone form). The semiquinone (FADH) can be formed by either reduction of FAD or oxidation of $FADH_2$ by accepting or donating one electron and one proton, respectively.

Feedback inhibition: The reaction is inhibited by final product of the same reaction. This is also known also end product inhibition.

Ferredoxin: A group of iron- and sulfur-containing proteins that function as electron carriers in photosynthetic and nitrogen-fixing organisms and in some anaerobic bacteria.

Ferredoxin-NADP reductase: An enzyme that receives electrons from ferredoxin in PSI and reduces $NADP^+$ to NADPH.

Fertilization: Fertilization is the union of the nucleus and other cellular constituents of a male gamete (sperm) with those of a female gamete (egg) to form a zygote. In gymnosperms fertilization may occur months after pollination. In angiosperms there is a double fertilization in which one of the two sperm nuclei from the pollen unites with the egg nucleus to form a diploid zygote and the other sperm nucleus unites with two of the nuclei of the embryo sac to form the triploid endosperm.

Fibrous: Seed with stringy or cord-like seed coat, as mace in Myristica.

Flaccid: A flaccid plant cell is one in which the plasma membrane is not pressed tightly against the cell wall. This is observed when the plant cell is placed in an isotonic solution wherein the concentration of solutes in the outside is the same as that in the inside of a plant cell.

Flooding stress: The partial or complete covering of plant or plant roots by water resulting in anaerobic stress is called as flooding stress. Availability of water to the plant is more than optimum requirement. The root will not get oxygen for respiration.

Flavoprotein: An enzyme with a flavin nucleotide (FMN or FAD) as tightly bound prosthetic group.

Florigen: Florigen (or **flowering hormone**) is the hypothesized hormone-like molecule responsible for controlling and/or triggering flowering in plants. Florigen is produced in the leaves, and acts in the shoot apical meristem of buds and growing tips.

Flowering locus C (FLC): This is gene coding for transcription factor responsible for repression of flowering in *Arabidopsis thaliana.*

Flowering response: The plants response to initiate flowering at particular time to the changing conditions like daylength, cold treatment etc. is called as flowering response.

Flowering: The transition of plant from vegetative growth to reproductive growth. Refers to the whole process from the flower induction to the floral evocation.

Fluid mosaic model: It explains the structure of biological membrane. It is explained by Singer and Nicholson. According to this model, any biological membrane is made of two layers of lipid layers arranged in a such a way that both sides of the membrane has hydrophilic head and interspersed with various proteins. Lipids maintain the fluidity of the membrane and proteins and other substances embedded on it gives a mosaic like appearance.

Fluence: The quantity of radiant energy falling on a small sphere, and can be expressed through photon fluence that measures the number of photons falling on the sphere and energy fluence that measures energy incident on the sphere.

Fluid mosaic model: A model describing biological membrane as fluid lipid bilayer with integral and peripheral proteins on it.

Fluorescence: Emission of light in the longer wavelength than incident light by exicited molecules leading to reversing back to ground state.

Field capacity: The amount of water retained by the soil after the drainage of gravitational water. This is the maximum water holding capacity of soil which will be high for clay soils and low for sand soils.

Framework elements: The essential elements that are constituents of organic substances which make about every chemical substance of life forms.

Free energy: Energy that is available in a system to do work is called as free energy.

Freeze avoidance: Lack of water crystallization in tissues at sub zero temperatures caused by the absence of either intrinsic or extrinsic nucleators. The tissue supercools and thereby escapes injury caused by ice formation.

Freeze dehydration: Loss of symplastic water caused by the vapor-pressure deficit created by ice in the extracellular spaces. The degree of dehydration is a function of temperature; as the temperature decreases, freeze-dehydration increases resulting in concentration of the cell contents.

Freeze tolerance: The ability of a cell or tissue to tolerate the presence of ice in the apoplastic spaces.

Freezing injury: Injury of biological material caused by sub-zero temperature.

Freezing point: The maximum temperature attained by the release of heat (exotherm) following the initiation of ice crystal formation. The temperature of ice crystal initiation may vary, depending on the presence of nucleating agents, but the freezing-point temperature is constant for any given solution.

Freezing stress: This stress occurs to plant at very low temperature especially less than 0°C and the temperature is low enough to form ice crystals inside the cell.

Freezing-point depression: The lowering of the freezing-point temperature of a solution by the presence of osmotically active compounds.

Frost heaving: Partial or complete uplifting of a surface caused by ice expansion and resulting in exposure and injury to plants.

Frost plasmolysis: Contraction of the dead protoplast from the cell wall following a lethal stress. Primarily due to the inability of the cell to reabsorb and maintain turgor following a lethal stress.

Frost protection: Methods of guarding against injury from temperature below 0 °C. Generally refers to protection of blossoms in the spring.

Fruit: Sweet and fleshy product of a tree or other plant which contains seeds. It is the ripened ovary of a plant and its contents.

Funicular: Seed with a persistent elongate funiculus attached to seed coat, as in Magnolia.

G

Gel: A semi-solid medium in to which proteins or nucleic acids are subjected to electrophoresis, to determine their size or to separate them from other components.

Gene family: A set of genes whose sequences differ only slightly that encode identical products; within a single species, a multigene family.

Gene tagging: The addition of a marker to a gene; often by the introduction of a transposon or insertion element.

Gene transfer: Transformation; the insertion of foreign DNA into a host conferring a trait not previously inherant in that organism.

Gene: The concise meaning might be the sequence of DNA that encodes a gene product (an RNA or protein), including all upstream and downstream sequences involved in the expression of the gene.

Genome: Sum of all genetic information of an organism, nucleus, organelle, or virus.

Geotropism (Barytropism or gravitropism): When a seedling is kept horizontally on the soil, the radicle always grows towards soil, and the plumule grows away from the soil. This type of growth movement of radicle and plumule is called positively geotropic and negatively geotropic respectively. But some runners and rhizomes grow parallel to the surface of the soil and this is referred to as diagiotropic. When the lateral roots grow obliquely into the soil, it is referred to as plagiogeotropic phenomenon.

Germination percentage: Germination percentage is an estimate of the viability of a population of seeds.

Germination percentage (GP) = (seeds germinated / total no. of seeds) × 100.

Germination: Germination is the process by which a plant grows from a seed. It is the protrusion of radical from seed coat at favourable conditions of a seed. The most common example of germination is the sprouting of a seedling from a seed of an angiosperm or gymnosperm. In addition, the growth of a sporeling from a spore, such as the growth of hyphae from fungal spores, is also germination.

Gibberellic acid: It is a class of Plant hormone. Gibberellins was first discovered by Kurosawa in diseased rice plants. The disease known as bakanae is caused by *Gibberella fujikuroi*. This fungi produces the GA and later it was isolated from plants. It has a role in germination of seeds, overcoming dormancy, synthesis of hydraulytic enzymes, bolting, formation of seedless fruits, internode elongation, etc.

Gibbs free energy (G): Free energy is the component of the total energy of a system that is available to do work.

Gluconeogenesis: Biosynthesis of carbohydrates from non-sugar precursors such as pyruvate or oxaloacetate which is basically through reversal of glycolysis.

Glucuronidase (GUS)**:** Bacterial enzyme encoded by the uidA gene; a selectable marker whose product can be directly visualized in many tissues.

Glutamate dehydrogenase (GDH): The enzyme involved in ammonium assimilation in plants reversibly catalysis conversion of alpha-ketoglutarate and ammonia to glutamate and vice versa.

Glutamate synthase: It is also known as GOGAT (Glutamine 2-oxoglutarate amino transferase). This enzyme transfers amide group from glutamine to 2-oxoglutarate forming two molecules of glutamate.

Glutamine synthetase (GS): The enzyme converts glutamate and ammonia into glutamine in the presence of ATP.

Glutathione: A tripeptide which act as coenzyme in many oxidation–reduction reactions in cells.

Glycine Betaine: N,N,N-trimethyl glycine. It is an important osmolyte which is synthesized during abiotic stress like drought and salinity and contribute for osmotic adjustment.

Glycolate metabolism: The biochemical cyclic pathway used by photo respiring plants for photo respiratory cation oxidation (PCO) that is accomplished in chloroplast, peroxisome and mitochondrion. This is due to oxygenase activity of Rubsico which produces one molecule of phosphoglyceric acid and one molecule of phosphoglycolate that enters into photorespiratory pathway.

Glycolysis: It is the initial step in both aerobic and anaerobic degradation of glucose in respiration. It is the breakdown of glucose (6 – carbon compound) into two molecules of pyruvic acid (3 – carbon compound). It happens in cytosol of the cell. The free energy released in this process is used to form the high energy compounds ATP and NADH.

Glycophytes: These plants do not grow in salt conditions. These plants are sensitive to excess salt in the soil or water.

Glyoxylate cycle: A variant of citric acid cycle that uses acetyl-CoA and two auxiliary enzymes to convert acetate into succinate and eventually a new carbohydrate. This occurs in few microorganisms and higher plants.

Glyoxysome: A cell organelle containing enzymes of glyoxylate cycle mainly found in plants tissues where fats are being actively converted into sugars such as germinating fatty seeds.

Gossypol: An aromatic sequiterpene dimer with 30- carbon, a secondary metabolite mainly found in cotton plant and provides resistance to insects, fungal and bacterial pathogens.

G-Protein: A GTP binding protein that is involved in signal transduction pathway. It act as molecular switch. G-protein transmit signal when bound to GTP and will have no effect when is bound to GDP.

Gravitational water: Gravitational water occurs only after a good rain or irrigation. Excess water is drained downwardly under the influence of gravity and joins ground water and this water is called gravitational water. This water is not available to the plants.

Gravitropism: Tropical movement in plants in response to gravity stimulus enabling roots to grow downward and stems to grow upward.

Green house effect: Warming of earth's due to trapping of long wave radiations by CO_2 and other hetero atomic gases in the atmosphere. This effect is similar to warming condition in green houses where the heat energy is trapped, hence it is named as green house effect.

Gross energy: It is defined as the total chemical energy (ATP) released or realized for complete oxidation of the food.

Growth analysis: In plants, growth analysis is an explanatory, holistic and integrative approach to interpret plant form and function. It uses simple primary data in the form of weights, areas, volumes and contents of plant components to investigate processes within and involving the whole plant.

Growth hormones: It is organic compound synthesized in one part of plant (site of synthesis) and translocated to another part to show its effect (site of action). At very low concentration especially in ppm concentration they causes physiological response. They are ubiquitous. They are Auxins Gibberellins, Cytokinin, Abscissic acid and Ethylene.

Growth inhibitors: Some organic substances produced in the plant that inhibits the plant growth. These substances are called growth inhibitors. They inhibit plant processes like seed germination, the elongation in roots, stems and leaves etc.

Growth movement: Irreversible curvature caused by differential growth; *i.e.*, plastic extension of cell walls, either differentially in a single cell on opposite flanks, or, in a multicellular organ, by differential cell growth on opposite flanks

Growth retardants: These compound are basically anti-gibberellins which reduce the elongation of stem thereby reducing the vegetative growth and convert into reproductive growth. *e.g.*, Paclobutrazol.

Growth: Growth can be defined as an irreversible permanent increase in size of an organ or its parts or even of an individual cell. Generally, growth is accompanied by metabolic processes.

Guard cells: It is modified epidermal cell present in leaf. It differ from other epidermal cells not only in the shape but also in the presence of chloroplast in them. Normally these are kidney shaped or dumb bell shaped.

Guttation: It is the process of water loss from plant in liquid form. It happens via hydathodes or water stomata. It is the exudation of drops of xylem sap on the tips or edges of leaves of some vascular plants, such as grasses. It happens because of root pressure.

Gycosidic bond: The bond between a sugar and other molecule through an intervening oxygen or nitrogen atom.

H

Half life: The time required for the disappearance of one half of a given component of a system.

Halochromism: It occurs when a substance changes color as the pH changes. This is a property of pH indicators, whose molecular structure changes upon certain changes in the surrounding pH. This change in structure affects a chromophore in the pH indicator molecule.

Halomorphic soil : A suborder of the intrazonal soil order, consisting of saline and sodic soils formed under imperfect drainage in arid regions and including the great soil groups Solonchak or Saline soils, Solonetz soils, and Soloth soils.

Hatch-Slack pathway: It is one of the carbon fixation pathway used by certain group of plants (C_4 plants) where the first stable compound is oxalo acetate, a C_4 dicarboxylic acid compound. In the first carboxylation reactions, atmospheric CO_2 combines with phosphoenol pyruvate (PEP) to oxalo acetate and then to malate. These plants posses kranz anatomy with mesophyll and bundle sheath cells.

Halophytes: These are plants which can tolerate salinity and grow.

Hardening: Conditioning or acclimation of an organism to a particular stress, which results in increased resistance to that stress and sometimes to other stresses. This term particularly used in tissue culture plants grown under shaded condition before it is used in open field.

Harvest Index: The harvest index is expressed as the percent ratio between the economic yield and total biological yield and was suggested by Nichiporovich (1951).

$$HI = (\text{Economic yield} / \text{Total biological yield}) \times 100$$

Heat of fusion: The enthalpy of fusion also known as (latent) heat of fusion is the change in enthalpy resulting from heating a given quantity of a substance to change its state from a solid to a liquid. The temperature at which this occurs is the melting point.

Heat of vapourisation: The heat of vaporization represents the amount of energy required to convert a unit volume of a liquid material to that of its gas.

Heme: A iron porphyrin prosthetic group of heme proteins such as hemoglobin and cytochromes.

Heat shock proteins: These are proteins produced by cells in response to high temperature to impart tolerance. The major functions include chaperons that facilitate the proper folding of proteins which is necessary for proper function. There are five classes of HSPs based on molecular weight.

Heavy metal stress: Metals like lead, aluminium creates toxicity to plants. It results in reducing metabolic activities of plant at cellular level and hence growth and development gets affected.

Heterotrophic: Organisms that cannot manufacture their own food, therefore it depends on other organism for its carbon source.

Heterotrimetric G-protein: A membrane bound GTP- binding protein consisting of three different subunits and involved in signal transduction pathway.

Heterogeneous solution: A heterogeneous mixture consists of visibly different substances or phases

Hexose Monophosphate shunt: It is a type of respiration (also called Phosphogluconate Pathway, or Hexose Monophosphate Shunt) parallel to glycolysis that generates NADPH and pentose as well as ribose 5 phosphate. This pathway is essential for nucleic acid synthesis.

High light stress: Light more than the optimum condition creates photo oxidation and photo inhibition in plants and hence growth and development process get affected. This type of stress is called as high light stress.

High temperature stress: In growing conditions of plant, when the temperature exceeds the optimum temperature for that particular species, then that temperature affects the normal growth processes in plants. This is referred as high temperature stress.

Hills reaction: See photolysis of water. This reaction is demonstrated by Robert Hill. It is the process in photosynthesis in which water gets splitted into proton, electron and oxygen because of strong oxidizing agent $P680^{+}$.

Hilum and funiculus: Funicular scar on seed coat that marks the point at which the seed was attached via the funiculus to the ovary tissue.

Histones: The family of five basic proteins tightly bound to DNA in chromosomes of eukaryotic cells.

Hoagland's solution: A standard nutrient solution for plant growth which are used for many crops especially for hydroponics system of cultivation.

Homogeneous solution: A homogeneous solution is a mixture of two or more components that have a uniform appearance and composition.

Homoiohydric: Plants that maintain a relatively constant level of hydration compared with large changes that occur in the water potential of their environment.

Holoenzyme: A complete enzyme including its prosthetic group and with full enzymatic activity. The enzyme without prosthetic group is known as apoenzyme.

Hormone binding proteins: A protein that binds the hormone in a saturable, specific manner.

Hormone receptor: A hormone binding protein that is shown to have a physiological effect after binding of the hormone.

Hydathodes: Hydathodes are specialized pores along the margins and apex of the leaf through which the secretion of water (guttation) takes place. Hydathodes or water stomata consists of vein endings, epithem, chamber and pores.

Hydroactive closure: Closure of stomata in response to water stress mediated through abcissic acid which is known to inhibit ATP driven H^+/K^+ ions exchange pumps in guard cells resulting in decreased solute content leading to loss of water from guards cells and stomatal closure.

Hydraulic conductance: Hydraulic conductance is a measure of the efficiency of bulk flow through a material, and defined as the flow rate per unit pressure driving force. The movement of water and dissolved substances through xylem is called hydraulic conductance.

Hydraulic conductivity: Hydraulic conductivity, symbolically represented as K, is a property of vascular plants, soils and rocks, that describes the ease with which a fluid (usually water) can move through pore spaces or fractures.

Hydrolysis: The chemical breakdown of a compound due to reaction with water. This is achieved by breaking a covalant bond by inserting a water molecules across the bond.

Hydrophyte: A plant adapted to environmental conditions of partial or full submersion in free water.

Hydroponics: The practice of growing plants in nutrient enriched water without soils is called as soil less growth or Hydroponics.

Hydrophobic : Non-polar or uncharged molecules or groups that are insoluble in water.

Hydrophillic: This is known as water loving molecules that are polar or charged molecules which dissolve in water.

Hypertonic solution: A hypertonic solution is a particular type of solution that has a high concentration of solutes on the outside of a cell when compared with the inside of a cell.

Hygrometer: An instrument to measure relative humidity of the atmosphere.

Hyper accumulation: Excessive accumulation of nutrients especially heavy metals in heavy metals tolerant plants without any deleterious effect on plant metabolism.

Hyper sensitive response (HR): This is the plant defense mechanism against microbial infection where host cells surrounding the infection site die rapidly to deprive the pathogen of nutrient supply and inhibiting spread in the host plant.

Hyponasty: Rapid growth of lower side of an organ leading to upward curling of leaf which is contrary to epinasty.

Hypocotyl: The axial part of the embryo between the cotyledons and the radicle. In seedlings, the juvenile stem which is seen between the cotyledons and the root system.

Hypogeal germination: The opposite of epigeal is hypogeal (underground germination).

Hypotonic solution: A solution that has a lower solute content therefore having high water potential or less negative water potential.

I

Ice nucleation: It is a process of reducing the formation of ice crystal under freezing stress, by some polysaccharides and proteins known as ice nucleators.

Imbibitions: It is a special type of diffusion when water is absorbed by solids-colloids-causing them to enormously increase in volume. The classical examples of imbibition are absorption of water by seeds and dry wood.

Immobile elements: The elements which get translocated slower inside the plant are called immobile elements. Examples: Ca, Fe and B.

Immunoassay: This is very sensitive method of identifying and or quantifying the hormones and other molecules which has antigen and antibody interaction.

Indeterminate growth: Plant growth in which the main stem continues to elongate indefinitely without being limited by a terminal inflorescence or other reproductive structure; also growth is characterized by sequential flowering from the lateral or basal buds to the central or uppermost buds.

Indole -3 acetic acid: It is naturally occurring auxin responsible for cell elongation, apical dominance and other physiological functions of auxins.

Induced dormancy: Induced dormancy in which dormancy develops as a response to external environmental factors.

Induced fit theory: It is conformational changes in an enzyme in response to its substrate binding leading to product formation. In this model, active site is modified based on substrate structure.

Inducible enzymes: The enzymes which are synthesized only in the presence of an inducer.

Inositol triphosphate: Triphosphate of a cyclic hexahydric alcohol known as inositol. This is act as a secondary messenger which trigger release of calcium from intracellular stores including vacuole.

Intercellular space: A space located or occurring between the cells is called inter cellular space.

Intermediate filaments: Important component of cytoskeleton especially in animals: a diverse group of helically wound structures with monomeric proteins. It has dimensions intermediate between actin filaments and microtubules.

Intermembrane space: The space between outer and inner membrane of a mitochondrion.

Internode elongation: It is the expansion of internodes (i.e part between two nodes). The cell in this region gets elongated resulting in increased length of internodes. The hormone GA has influence in internode elongation.

Intracellular space: A space located or occurring outside the cells or cell wall is called intracellular space.

Inulin: A storage polysaccharide, a fructosan consisting of about 30 fructofuranose units joined together by glycosidic linkage.

Ion channel: An integral membrane protein that provides regulated transport of a specific ion or ions across the membrane.

Ionic stress: This stress is due to excess ions in the tissue.

Ionophore: A compound that binds with one or more metal ions and is capable of crossing the membrane along bound ion. Most of them are produced by microorganisms. e.g., Vallinomycin and gramicidin.

Irradiance: Radiance flux per unit area reaching a surface. Measured in watts per square metre (Wm^{-2}).

Iso-electric point: The pH at which a substance such as protein has no net electric charge and thus does not move in an electric field.

Isomerase: The enzymes that catalyses the isomerisation reactions.

Isoprene: The hydrocarbon, 5C unit with branched carbon skeleton and is recurring unit of terpenoid biomolecules.

Isothermal: Occurring at constant temperature.

Isotonic solution: If the external solution balances the osmotic pressure of the cytoplasm it is said to be isotonic solution. If a cell placed in isotonic solution there is no movement of solution from cell to outside solution to cell.

Isotopes: Atoms of same element with same atomic number but different atomic weights may be stable or radioactive.

Isozymes: Multiple forms of an enzyme catalyzing the same biochemical reactions but have different molecular structure and kinetic properties.

J

Jasmonic acid: Jasmonic acid is derived from the fatty acid, linolenic acid. It is a member of the jasmonate class of plant hormones. It is biosynthesized from linolenic acid by the octadecanoid pathway. The major function of JA and its various metabolites is regulating plant responses to abiotic and biotic stresses as a well as plant growth and development processes.

Javorization: The word javorize is a verb which means to stimulate growth of a plant by shortening its rest period. An example of javorize is to keep orchids in the green house during the cold winter. It is the other name of the vernalization.

K

Ketose: A simple sugar in which carbonyl group is a ketone.

Kinases: Enzymes that catalyse phosphorylation of an acceptor molecule such as protein molecule by ATP.

Kinesins: This is a group of microtubule based motor proteins formed from multicomponent complexes that are involved in organelle transport in eukaryotic cells.

Kinetin: This is 6-amino furfuryl purine compound belongs to synthetic cytokinins.

Kleptoplasty: It is unique symbiotic relationship phenomenon where plastids from algae are sequestered by host organism. This is found in molluscs, the green sea slugs.

Kranz anatomy: 'Kranz' in German means wreath. In leaves, sheath of cells having chloroplast are radially arranged surrounding the vascular bundles and look like a ring or wreath. The cells of bundle sheath cells in such plants are therefore also called as Kranz cells. It is a specialized structure of C_4 plants leaf anatomy.

Krebs cycle: One of the respiratory cycle after the glycolysis where pyruvic acid is converted into acetyl coA and entered into krebs cycle. In this cycle, there is regeneration of NADH and FADH2 which are then oxidized in the mitochondrial electron transport chain.

L

Lactate dehydrogenase: An enzyme that reversibly catalyses conversion of pyruvate to lactate by utilizing NAD as coenzyme. This operates under anaerobic respiratory condition.

Lactate fermentation: Lactic acid fermentation is a biological process by which glucose and six carbon sugars (also, disaccharides of six carbon sugars, e.g. sucrose or lactose) are converted into cellular energy and the metabolite lactate. It is an anaerobic fermentation reaction.

Latent heat: The heat required to convert a solid into a liquid or vapour, or a liquid into a vapour, without change of temperature. It is also called as hidden heat.

Leaching requirement: (LR) The amount of water in excess of the plant requirement that is needed to remove salt from the root zone in order to prevent soil salinity from exceeding a specified value.

Leaf Area Duration (LAD): It is the functional leaf area or estimated photosynthetic area which contributed for the total biomasss. To correlate dry matter yield with Leaf area, Power *et al.,* (1967) integrated the Leaf area with time and called as Leaf Area Duration. LAD taken into account, both the duration and extent of photosynthetic tissue of the crop canopy. The LAD is expressed in m^2. days.

Leaf Area Index (LAI): Williams (1946) proposed the term, Leaf Area Index (LAI). It is the ratio of the leaf of the crop to the ground area over a period of interval of time. The value of LAI should be optimum at the maximum ground cover area at which crop canopy receives maximum solar radiation and hence, the total dry matter will be high.

Leaf Area Ratio (LAR): The term, Leaf Area Ratio (LAR) was suggested by Radford (1967). Leaf area per unit plant biomass ($cm^2\ g^{-1}$). LAR is a measure of the proportion of the plant which is engaged in photosynthetic process. It gives the relative size of the assimilatory apparatus. It is defined as the ratio between leaf area in square centimeters and total plant dry weight. It represents leafiness character of crop plants on area basis.

Leaf Area: It is the space covered by the leaf. This is the area of photosynthetic surface produced by the individual plant over a period of interval of time and expressed in $cm^2\ plant^{-1}$.

Leaf concentrate: Leaf concentrate is an extremely nutritious food produced by coagulating the juice of certain fresh green leaves. The process of removing most of the water and fiber transforms dark green leaves into a more concentrated, more digestible, and more adaptable food. Leaf concentrate is sometimes known as leaf protein, leaf protein concentrate, leaf nutrient or leaf extract.

Leaf expansion: The process in which the cells in the leaf get expands so that finally the size of the leaf gets increased.

Leaf fall: Shedding of leaves by plants. The natural separation and dropping of the leaf at the end of the growing season over a short period in deciduous plants or intermittently throughout the year in coniferous trees.

Leaf folding: It is a mechanism by which plants fold their leaves inorder to avoid transpiration so that it can survive under water limited conditions. Sometimes leaves gets folded even in mid day water deficit conditions. It is one of the drought avoidance mechanism.

Leaf rolling: It is a mechanism by which plants roll their leaves in order to avoid transpiration so that it can survive under water limited conditions. It is one of the drought avoidance mechanisms.

Leaf Weight Ratio (LWR): It was coined by (Kvet *et al.,* 1971). It is the leaf weight per unit plant biomass. It is defined as the ratio between grams of dry matter in leaves and total dry matter in plants (g). Since the numerator and denominator are on dry weight basis LWR is dimensionless. It is the index of leafiness of the plant on weight basis.

Lectins: Protein that recognize and reversibly bind with specific carbohydrates. The lectin ricin from castor bean is one of the powerful animal toxins known. In legumes, it is important for establishing symbiotic relationship with bacteria in nitrogen fixation.

Leghemoglobin: An oxygen binding heme protein found in root nodules of legumes. It is important for regulation of oxygen supply to bacteroids and protects the nitrogenase that is sensitive to oxygen.

Lenticular transpiration: The loss of water in the form of water vapour taking place through the lenticels present in woody stem and fruits.

Ligases: Enzymes those catalyses the linking of two molecules coupled with the breakdown of pyrophosphate bond of ATP or similar other triphosphate.

Light compensation point: The light intensity at which the rate of CO_2 uptake for photosynthesis is equal to rate of CO_2 release for respiration.

Light extinction coefficient: Extinction coefficient refers to the measure of light in a medium. Light extinction coefficient in relation to plants refers to the amount of light absorbed by the canopy of plant when light passes through the canopy. It is the ratio of light intercepted by crop between the top and bottom of crop canopy to the LAI.

Light harvesting complex: The complexes which are involved in light reaction of photosynthesis and these are involved in absorption of light and passing onto the reaction center chlorophyll molecule.

Light reaction: Light Reaction is the process of reactions occurs in the thylakoid membrane. They include light absorption, water splitting, oxygen formations and the formation of high energy chemical intermediate ATP and NADPH. It is also called as Hydrogen Transfer Phase.

Light Transmission Ratio (LTR): It is expressed as the ratio of quantum of light intercepted by crop canopy at top to the bottom. Light intensity is expressed in K lux or Wm^{-2}

Lignin: A highly complex and branched polymer of phenyl propanoid alcohols present mainly in secondary walls of supporting and conducting tissues especially tracheids and vessels of xylem of all vascular plants.

Lipases: Enzymes that catalyses hydrolysis of triglycerides.

Lipid: One of primary metabolites or macro molecule insoluble in water but soluble in organic solvents which includes fatty acids, waxes, sterols.

Lock and key theory: Theory that explains the interaction of substrate and enzymes in a specific manner as that of specific key fits to lock. The theory is proposed by H. Emil Fischer (1985) which is accepted to explain the enzyme action.

Long day plants: The plants that flowers only after being exposed to light period longer than critical length, *e.g.,* Spinach, lettuce and some varieties of wheat.

Long distance transport: Translocation of solutes through phloem from source to sink by the pressure flow known as munch hypothesis.

Low light stress: Light is not sufficient to plant in this type of stress. It affects the photosynthesis.

Lycopene: It is carotenoids that is widely distributed in photosynthetic bacteria and also characteristics of tomato, tetraterpene with the molecular formula of $C_{40}H_{56}$.

Lysases: The enzyme catalysing reactions in which either a double bond is established due to removal of a group from a molecule or a group is added to the double bond.

Lysosome: A cell organelle in the eukaryotic cells that contains hydrolytic enzymes to breakdown the proteins that are targeted to that organelle. Lysosomes are usual feature of animals cells.

M

Macromolecule: A molecule having molecular weight ranging from few thousand to millions.

Macronutrients: The essential elements which are required by plants in comparatively large amounts are called as major elements or macro nutrients. Examples: C, H, O, N, P, K, Ca, S, Mg. In this C, H, O, N, P, K are called primary elements and Ca, S, Mg are called as secondary elements.

Malate shuttle: A mechanism of transferring reducing equivalent of cytosolic NADH in the form of malate across the inner mitochondrial membrane by a specific ketoglutarate malate transporter for oxidation through electron transport chain in little animal tissue like heart muscle.

Malic enzyme: An enzyme that catalyzes the oxidation of malate to pyruvate and carbondioxide.

Malting: First process in the brewing process to enhance production of beer using germinated barley seeds through hydrolytic enzymes.

Mangroves: Group of woody plants (about 11 genera) that grows in saline aquatic habitats (e.g., marine estuaries and swamps) and is capable of tolerating sea water. Common genera include *Avicennia* and *Rhizophora.*

Mass flow: Flow of solutes along with solvents is called as mass flow. In the process, ions or salts move along with water. An accepted model of phloem transport proposed by E. Munch wherein sugar transport in phloem is driven by osmotically generated pressure gradient between source and sink.

Matric potential (ψ_m)**:** A component of water potential due to the adhesion of water molecules to non-dissolved structures of the system, i.e. the matrix, such as plasma membranes or soil particles. It is always negative and is significant only outside living cells in relatively dry systems, for example soils, where much of the water is tightly bound to soil particles.

Matrix: In biology, matrix (plural: matrices) is the material (or tissue) in animal or plant cells, in which more specialized structures are embedded, and a specific part of the mitochondrion. The inner cavity of mitochondria is filled with a watery solution containing one of the needed materials of Kreb cycle.

Mechanical dormancy: Mechanical dormancy occurs when seed coats or other coverings are too hard to allow the embryo to expand during germination.

Megapascals (MPa): 10^6 pascals equal to 10 bars or 9.87 atmosphere. This is unit for expression of water potential, osmotic potential and pressure potential of plants.

Meiosis: Meiosis is a process of cell division in which the genetic content or the number of chromosomes in a cell divides into 2 equal halves. This division is called reduction division. This division occurs in gametic cells.

Melting point depression: The decrease in the temperature needed to melt a solid (e.g., ice) due to the addition of solutes.

Membrane fluidity: A property of membranes determined by fatty acid chain length, saturation level and sterol components.

Membrane integrity: Role of membrane around the cell or cell organelle is to act as a barrier and regulation of solute entry in and out of the cell. Exposure to any stress, breaks the integrity of the plasma membrane and hence the membrane would not do its function and this can kill the affected cell.

Membrane permeability: The facilitated transport of a molecule across the membrane through a specific membrane protein. The extent to which a membrane allows or restricts entry of substances through it.

Meristem: Region of growth zone in which cell division occurs rapidly accompanied by cell enlargement.

Mesocotyl: The first internode between scutellum (single cotyledons) and the case of coleoptiles in germinating seedling of a grass seed or cereal grain.

Mesophyte: A plant adapted to environmental conditions of moderate water availability.

Messenger RNA (mRNA): The complementary stand of DNA which carries message from DNA to protein. It is intermediate product in the central dogma of life.

Metabolism: The sum total of the enzymatic reactions (anabolism and catabolism together) that occur in living cells.

Metabolite: A chemical substance which takes part in or formed by metabolic reactions in living cells. It is also an intermediate or final product of metabolic reactions.

Metabolome: The entire pool of metabolites present within a living cell, tissue or an organism under defined condition such as a particular physiological or developmental state excluding macro molecules.

Metabolomics: The study of entire pool of metabolites in living cells and how this metabolites changes under different physiological, environmental or developmental conditions.

Michaelis-menton constant (Km): The substrate concentration at which the rate of reactions is one half of the maximum capacity.

Microbodies: Membrane bound vesicles in cytoplasm of eukaryotic cells that contain peroxide forming and peroxide destroying enzymes including glyoxysomes and peroxisomes.

Microfibrils: Microfibril is a very fine fibril like strand, consisting of glycoproteins and cellulose.

Microfilaments: It is the assemebly of globular proteins and one type of cytoskeleton elements found in plants.

Microtubules: It is another type of cytoskeleton elements and non-membraneous elongated hollow cylindrical structure made up of globular proteins as that of microfilaments.

Micronutrients: The essential elements which are required in very small amounts or traces by the plants are called minor elements or micronutrients or trace elements. e.g., Zn , Mn, B ,Cl, Cu,and Mo.

Micropyle: Micropyle is a small opening in the surface of an ovule, through which the pollen tube penetrates, often visible as a small pore in the ripe seed. In seeds, micropyle is a tiny pore in the testa opposite the tip of the radicle. It admits water to the embryo before active germination.

Middle lamella: Thin layer of cells made up of calcium pectate that is between adjacent cell and is between two primary cell walls of adjacent cells.

Mineral elements: Any chemical element required by an organism for healthy growth.

Mineral nutrition: The study of how plants obtain, distribute, metabolize and utilize mineral nutrients is called as Mineral nutrition.

Mineral toxicity: The term mineral toxicity refers to a condition in which the concentration in the plant tissue of any one of the minerals necessary for normal growth and developmental process is abnormally high, and which has an adverse effect on plant growth.

Minerals: Minerals are substances that are formed naturally in the Earth. Minerals are usually solid, inorganic, have a crystal structure, and form naturally by geological processes.

Mitochondria: An organelle found in large numbers in most cells, in which the biochemical process of respiration and energy production occur. It has double membrane, the inner part being folded inwards to form layers. It is called as powerhouse of cell.

Mitochondrial electron transport chain: The stage of cellular respiration in which the most adenosine triphosphate is generated. In this biochemical reaction, electrons are passed along the cytochromes of a cell or mitochondrial membrane and are ultimately accepted by oxygen, producing water. Hydrogen ions (protons) are transported across the membrane. The source of the protons and electrons is primarily nicotinamide adenine dinucleotide, which is recycled during the reaction.

Mitosis: Mitosis is process of cell division by which a cell replicates itself into two similar copies to produce two daughter cells and this division occurs in all vegetative cells of plant.

Mobile elements: The element which travels fast inside plant are called mobile elements. Examples: N, P, K, S and Mg.

Molar Solutions: A one molar solution is a solution in which 1 mole of a compound is dissolved in a total volume of 1 litre or one gram molecular weight of substance dissolved in 1000 mL. For example: The molecular weight of sodium chloride (NaCl) is 58.44, so one gram molecular weight (= 1 mole) is 58.44g.

Monocarpic biennials: The plants that is monocarpic flowers once, set seeds, and dies. However biennials may flower in their second growing season, but usually take longer in the field. e.g., Carrot.

Monocarpic plants: Monocarpic plants are those that flower, set seeds and then die. They flower only once in their life time.

Monocot seed: Subclass of angiosperms characteristic by having only one cotyledon in the embryo. Differ from dicotyledons in a number of morphological characters like leaf, root and stem structure. Examples for woody monocotyledons are bamboos and palms.

Monoterpene: It belongs to one of secondary metabolites, terpenoids and made up of two isoprene units with ten carbon.

Mottling: An area of skin composed of varying shades or colors.

Mouse ear: Mouse ear is the deficiency of certain micro nutrient like nickel in pecan plants.

Mucigel: A slimy viscous substance, a highly hydrated complex polysaccharide secreted by root of plants which helps to lubricate passage of growing root tip through the soil.

Mucilage: Mucilage is a gelatinous substance of various plants (as legumes or seaweeds) that contains protein and polysaccharides and is similar to plant gums.

Mucopolysaccharide: The polysaccharide which contains aminosugars or their derivatives such as chitin.

Mutant: A gene that undergone mutation within the particular organism by different means of mutation leading alteration in the phenotype.

Mutation: A change in nucleotide sequence in the DNA or gene leading to genetically inheritable alterations.

MYB proteins: It is a class of transcription factors which can bind to promoters and activate the genes. This kind of transcription factors implicated in GA signaling pathways.

Mycorrhiza: A fungus which has symbiotic relationship with plants and helps in absorption of nutrients from the soil to the plants.

N

NAD/NADP (Nicotinamide Adenine Dinucleotide/ Nicotinamide Adenine Dinucleotide Phosphate): Coenzymes acting as carriers of hydrogen atoms and electrons in some oxidoreductases catalyzed reactions. Their oxidized and reduced states are NAD^+ and $NADH + H^+$/$NADP^+$ and $NADPH + H^+$

Nanotechnology: Nanotechnology refers broadly to a field of applied science and technology whose unifying theme is the control of matter on the molecular level in scales smaller than 1 micrometre, normally 1 to 100 nanometers, and the fabrication of devices within that size range.

Nastic movement: Nastic movements are non-directional responses to stimuli (*e.g.*, temperature, humidity, light irradiance), and are usually associated with plants. The movement can be due to changes in turgor or changes in growth. An example of such a response is opening and closing of flowers. There are several types of nastic movements such as Epinasty, Hyponasty, Photonasty, Nyctinasty, Chemonasty, Hydronasty, Thermonasty, Geonasty/Gravinasty, Thigmonasty, etc.

Necrosis: It is the form of cell injury which results in the premature death of cells in living tissue by autolysis.

Necrotic spots: Small spots of dead tissues in plants, usually caused by some mineral nutrient deficiency.

Nernst equation: An equation which predicts the electric potential at which a charged ion will be in equilibrium across a membrane, as a function of the relative concentration of the ion on each side of the membrane.

Net Assimilation Rate (NAR): The term, NAR was used by Williams (1946). NAR is defined as dry matter increment per unit leaf area per unit of time.

The NAR is a measure of the average photosynthetic efficiency of leaves in a crop community. NAR is expressed as the grams of dry weight increase per unit leaf area per unit time (g. $m^{-1}day^{-1}$)

$$NAR = \frac{(W_2 - W_1)(\log_e LA_2 - \log_e LA_1)}{(T_2 - T_1)(LA_2 - LA_1)}$$

Where W_1 = dry weight of initial sampling and W_2 = dry weight of final sampling

LA_1 = leaf area at T_1 and LA_2 = Leaf area at T_2

Net primary productivity: It is the total amount of carbon assimilated by photosynthesis minus the amount of carbon lost through respiration.

Nif genes: Nitrogen fixing genes in bacteria; a set of 17 genes comprising seven or eight operons each transcribing usually a polycistronic m-RNA.

Night interruption (night break or light break): With reference to inhibition or promotion of some photoperiodic response by interrupting the dark period with an interval of light. Depending upon species, the light break will be more or less effective depending upon when it is given and upon the irradiance level and the spectral quality.

Long-day plants typically require a much longer period of interruption at a higher irradiance level than do short-day plants. If the light break is effective, it acts as a long-day treatment (promoting a long-day response or inhibiting a short-day response). Response to a night interruption is an excellent test for a true photoperiodic response.

Nitrate reductase: Conversion of nitrate (NO_3^-) to nitrite (NO_2^-) is catalyzed by enzyme, nitrate reductase.

Nitrification: Conversion of ammonia to nitrite (No_2^-) and then nitrate (No_3^-) is known as nitrification. Nitrifying bacteria like nitrosomonas convert ammonia to nitrite and another bacterium called Nitrobacter converts nitrite to nitrate.

Nitrite reductase: Conversion of nitrite (NO_3^-) to ammonia is catalyzed by enzyme, nitrite reductase.

Nitrogen cycle: It is the cyclic process of fixing of atmospheric molecular nitrogen into nitrogenous compounds, their circulation through various organisms and finally release of molecular nitrogen back into atmosphere by various means.

Nitrogen fixation: Nitrogen fixation is a process by which nitrogen in the Earth's atmosphere is converted into ammonia (NH_3) or other molecules available to living organisms.

Nitrogenase enzyme: Nitrogen fixing bacteria possess a nitrogenase enzyme complex that catalyses the reduction of molecular nitrogen to ammonia.

Night length: Dark period in a natural 24-hour cycle of light and darkness, as this might influence plant growth or development.

Nod factors: Rhizobia in soil will secrete these which are usually chitin derivatives in order to prepare the host roots for invasion.

Nod genes (nodulation genes): Genes of Rhizobia that encode for proteins which contribute to nodule formation.

Nod genes (Nodulin genes): Plant (host) genes specific to nodule formation.

Nodules: Specialised tubercle like structures on the surface of roots of host plant that contain symbiotic nitrogen fixing bacteria.

Nodule formation: Root nodules occurs on the root of the plants that associates with symbiotic nitrogen fixing bacteria under nitrogen limiting condition, capable plant form a symbiotic relationship with a host specific strain of bacteria.

Non-competitive inhibition: A type of inhibition of enzyme activity, in which the inhibition is not reversed by increasing the substrate concentration of that enzyme. So it is irreversible inhibition.

Non-mineral element: Any substance occurring in nature, usually comprising inorganic substance as quartz or felspar, of definite chemical composition and usually of definite crystal structure, but sometimes also including rocks formed by these as well as certain natural products of organic origin as asphalt or coal.

Non-cyclic electron transport (Z-scheme): Light induced flow of electrons from Water to $NADP^+$ involving both the photosystems I and II.

Non-cyclic photophosphorylation: Non-Cyclic Photophosphorylation is defined as the process of production of ATP and $NADPH^+$. This is one type of photosynthetic electron transport chain. This process of electron transport involves both Photosystem I and Photosystem II which act in tandem and is initiated by the absorption of a photon of light by Reaction centre chlorophyll molecule of P680. The electron flows from water to NADP.

Non-endospermic seeds: The cotyledons serve as sole food storage organs as in the case of pea (*Pisum sativum*). During embryo development the cotyledons absorb the food reserves from the endosperm. The endosperm is almost degraded in the mature seed and the embryo is enclosed by the testa.

Non-heme iron proteins: Proteins containing iron that is not associated with porphyrin group. Involved in many oxidation-reduction reactions.

Non-polar (Hydrophobic): Groups or molecules sparingly soluble in water.

Non-protein amino acids: A large group of over 200 amino acids which occur free in cells and are not incorporated into proteins.

Non-reducing sugars: Sugars which does not have open functional groups or sugars without free aldehyde or keto group and hence it can't reduce cupric ions to cuprous ions.

Nonsense codon: Also called as termination codons. These codons will not specify any amino acids because the occurrence of these codons will signal for termination of polypeptide chains.

Nonsense DNA: Genetic error that results in premature termination of transcription into RNA.

Normal Solutions: A one normal solution is a solution in which one gram equivalent weight of substance dissolved in 1000 mL.

Northern blot: The hybridization on a membrane of a specific radiolabeled probe with RNA transferred from an electrophoretic separation.

NPA (Naphthyl phthalamic acid): Inhibitor of polar transport of auxin.

Nucleoid: Region of a prokaryote, plastid, or mitochondrion where DNA is concentrated.

Nucleolus: A dense spherical structure in nucleus in eukaryotic cells that is visible during interphase and also site of ribosomal RNA (r-RNA) synthesis.

Nucleoside: The basic subunit of DNA and RNA, composed of base (A, T or U, G, C) joined to a pentose sugar.

Nucleosome: Structural unit for packaging chromatin in which small stretch of duplex DNA is wrapped around a bead of histones.

Nucleotide: The basic subunit of DNA and RNA, composed of a base (A, T or U, G, C), a sugar (deoxyribose or ribose), and a phosphate.

Nucleus: The portion of the cell, often membrane bound, that contains the chromatin.

Null-response technique: An approach used in studies on photoperiodic phenomena and on other photobiological responses in which irradiance levels of two opposing wavelengths (*i.e.*, red and far-red in most applications) are balanced to produce the same plant response as would be produced by darkness or by some white light source.

Nutation: Autonomous growth movement over extended periods, *i.e.*, curvature of organs (or change of curvature), caused by differential flank growth, which is not induced by an external stimulus.

Nutrient: A substance needed to survive or necessary for the synthesis of organic compounds in plants.

Nutrition: The process of obtaining the food necessary for growth and development. It might be the organic and inorganic nutrient salts necessary for plant growth and development.

Nutrient depletion zone: The area of soil from where roots are able to extract mineral nutrients.

Nutrient solution: A solution containing essential macro and micro nutrients by dissolving inorganic salts in specific concentration for growth of plants in sunlight without soil or organic matter.

Nyctinasty: A diurnal periodic upward and downward movement, usually of leaves or petioles, mainly controlled by the physiological clock but, in addition, synchronized by an external factor. Sometimes not restricted to autonomous movements, but used also for movements that are induced by rhythmic light-dark changes, or only those that are induced by light-dark transition in the sense of scotonasty.

O

Obligate photoperiodism: Obligate photoperiod plants absolutely require a long or short day before flowering. If required photoperiod condition is not met they won't flower. This phenomenon is called obligate photoperiodism.

Oleosome (Spherosome or oil body): Cell organelle bounded by a single membrane and contains triglycerides.

Oligohalophyte: A plant adapted to habitats of low salinity (0.04 to 0.4 MPa at field capacity; EC 1 to 10 dS/m).

Oligomycin: An antibiotic that inhibits oxidative phosphorylation by blocking the activity of F_0F_1 ATP synthase.

Oligosaccharide: A molecule containing fewer number of monosaccharide units joined by glycosidic bonds.

Omega oxidation (ω-oxidation): Oxidation of fatty acid, in which initial oxidation occurs at the carbon atom which is farthest from the carboxylic group.

One-instant mechanism (spatial sensing of direction): The direction of stimulus is sensed at one instant by comparing the arriving stimulus at two (or more) receptor sites.

Operculum: A little seed lid. It refers to a dehiscent cap of a seed or a fruit that opens during germination.

Operon: A unit of genetic expression consisting of one or more contiguous genes that are coordinately regulated by a promoter and an operator in prokaryotic cells.

Optical activity: The property of molecule to rotate the plane polarized light. Chirality of the molecule is necessary for optical activity.

Optically Active Isomers: Names of chiral compounds whose absolute configuration is known may be differentiated by the prefixed R- and S-

Optimum temperature: Optimum temperature is responsible for maximizing the growth of plant and thus the yield of the plants. Even more or less availability affects the plants and it leads to the death of that particular plant.

Ordinary companion cell: A type of companion cells connected by surrounding cells other than sieve elements, by fewer plasmodesmata.

Organic elements: The elements that can be synthesized in the plant system.

Organogenesis: Formation of new organs such as shoot and root from tissue or cell is known as organogenesis.

Orthodox seed: Orthodox seeds are seeds which will survive drying and/or freezing during ex-situ conservation.

Osmolality: Total sum of all osmotic potentials caused by total solutes dissolved in cell sap regardless of molecular species.

Osmoregulants: The solute which is produced inside the cell of some plants to regulate the osmotic process of water absorption from soil. It increase solute concentration in a cell. It should be easily soluble in water. It should not carry any charges. It should disintegrate rapidly. Plants which produces these solutes in response to abiotic stress are said to have tolerance towards stress and grow relatively well in stressful conditions. Also known as osmolytes, compatible solutes or osmoprotectants.

Osmoregulation: Partial or complete maintenance of cell turgor over a range of total water potentials by regulated changes in cell osmotic potential. This process is well documented in the turgor and volume maintenance of certain algal species when exposed to changes in the osmotic potential of their aqueous environment.

Osmosis: Movement of molecules from higher concentration to lower concentration through a semipermeable membrane until the equilibrium is reached.

Osmosis (in terms of water potential): Movement of water from higher water potential to lower water potential through a semi-permeable membrane until the equilibrium is reached.

Osmotic adjustment: Changes in concentration of certain cell solutes in response to changes in cell water potential. These changes contribute to osmoregulation.

Osmotic concentration: Formerly known as Osmolarity, is the measure of solute concentration defined as the number of osmoles of solute per litre (L) of solution (osmol/L or Osm/L).

Osmotically generated flow: Flow that arises from negative osmotic potential within sieve tubes (phloem translocation) or xylem vessels (root pressure, root exudation, guttation).

Osmotic potential (Y_s): It also called solute potential. When solute particles are added to pure solvent, the water potential decreases, because the dissolutions of solutes lowers the total number of free molecules of water and also the free energy of solvent.

Osmotic pressure (OP): Osmotic Pressure is the minimum pressure which needs to be applied to a solution to prevent the inward flow of its pure solvent across a semipermeable membrane.

Osmotic-potential gradient: The difference in osmotic potential in a file of sieve elements over a specified distance of phloem path which decides the movement of solute in phloem.

Osmotic shock: Osmotic stress caused by a sudden and drastic change in external osmotic potential.

Osmotic stress: Osmotic stress is a sudden change in the solute concentration around a cell, causing a rapid change in the movement of water across its cell membrane. Under conditions of high concentrations of either salts, substrates or any solute in the supernatant water is drawn out of the cells through osmosis.

Osmoticum: A solute that decreases osmotic potentials of cell solutions as its concentration increases (i.e., any solute).

Ovules: Ovules are structures of seed plants containing the female gametophyte with the egg cell, all being surrounded by the nucellus and 1-2 integuments.

Oxidation: Oxidation is the loss of electrons from an atom or molecule or substance. The chemical process by which starches and sugars are converted into energy. Controlled oxidation in living cells is called respiration.

Oxidative phosphorylation: The process in which ATP is synthesized in Mitochondrial Electron Transport chain oxidizing the NADH in mitochondria.

Oxido-reductases: Enzymes catalyzing oxidation-reduction reaction.

Oxidative stress: Stress created by reactive oxygen species or free radicals of oxygen such as singlet oxygen, superoxide, hydrogen peroxide and hydroxyl radicals is called as oxidative stress. Electron transport chains are major sites of premature electron leakage to oxygen generating superoxide and potentially resulting in increased oxidative stress. It is essentially an imbalance between the production of free radicals and the ability to contract or detoxify their harmful effects through neutralization by antioxidants.

Oxygenases: Enzymes which adds oxygen to the substrate.

Oxygen evolving complex (OEC): A small complex of proteins and manganese ions associated with reaction center of photosystem II which splits water molecules to yield molecular oxygen during photosynthesis.

Oxygenic organisms: The organisms which evolve oxygen during photosynthesis.

P

P680: Reaction center chlorophyll in Photosystem II (PSII) which absorbs maximum light of 680 nm in its neutral state.

P700: Reaction center chlorophyll in Photosystem I (PSI) which absorbs maximum light of 700 nm in its neutral state.

P870: Form of bacteriochlorophyll in reaction center of pigment system in photosynthetic purple bacteria that absorbs light maximally at 870 nm in its neutral state.

Paclobutrazol: It is a chemical compound which inhibits Gibberellin biosynthesis. It is also a growth retardant commercially used in overcoming alternate bearing of mango.

Palindrome: Inverted repeats of DNA such that the sequence is the same when read forward or backward; *e.g.*, CAGTTGAC, or in the English language, "Madam, I'm Adam."

Palisade Parenchyma : Palisade parenchyma cells are seen beneath the upper epidermis. It consists of vertically elongated cylindrical cells in one or more layers. These cells are compactly arranged without intercellular spaces. Palisade parenchyma cells contain more chloroplasts than the spongy parenchyma cells. The function of palisade parenchyma is photosynthesis.

Pantothenic acid (Vitamin B_5): An important constituent of coenzyme A which is involved in transacylation reactions.

PAPS (3' phosphoadenosine 5' phosphosulphate): A coenzyme that is carrier of sulphate group.

Paraheliotropic: Orienting parallel to the incident solar radiation. Paraheliotropic leaf movements in plants under water stress reduces intercepted radiation and can reduce leaf temperature and leaf transpiration.

Parastichy: In phyllotaxis, a helical or spiral arrangement of leaves or scales along a stem or around the center of a shoot apical meristem.

Parenchyma cells: Parenchyma cells are alive at maturity. They function in storage, photosynthesis, and as the bulk of ground and vascular tissues. Spongy parenchyma and Palisade parenchyma cells are elongated cells located in many leaves just below the epidermal tissue.

Parthenocarpy: Parthenocarpy is the natural or artificially induced production of fruit without fertilization of ovules. The fruit is therefore seedless.

Parthenogenesis: Parthenogenesis is the process of reproduction from an unfertilized egg which is a type of apomixis.

Partitioning: A Distribution of translocated photoassimilates among sinks.

Pascal (Pa): SI unit of pressure, equal to the force of one newton per square meter (Nm^{-2}).

Passage cells: Thin walled unsuberized cells found in the endodermis of vascular plants often opposite the protoxylem strands.

Passive absorption: Absorption of nutrient or ions or water without spending of energy is called as passive absorption.

Passive transport: Movement of solute across the membrane in the direction of electrochemical gradient from higher to lower potential.

Pasteur's effect: A slowing or complete cessation of alcoholic fermentation in the presence of oxygen is called as Pasteur effect. It was first observed by C. Pasteur. This occurs in animal and plant tissues where oxygen inhibits aerobic glycolysis.

Patatin: It is a family of glycoproteins present in potato tubers. It accounts to 30–40% of total soluble proteins. These proteins also have lipase activity and can cleave fatty acids from membrane lipids; a cause for potato allergy.

Patch clamp technique: A technique by which electrophysiological measurements of currents through ion channels in the cell membrane is made.

Pathogenesis related proteins (PR proteins): These are defense proteins synthesized by plants in response to the microbial or pathogen attack and by which it check the growth of pathogens.

PCD (Programmed cell death): *See* Apoptosis

PCO (Photorespiratory carbon oxidation): *See* photorespiration

PCR (Photosynthetic carbon reduction pathway): *See* Calvin cycle

Pectins: A heterogeneous group of polysaccharides consisting of an arabinan, a galactan and a galacturonan that are important constituents of middle lamellae and primary cell wall of higher plants.

Pendulum timer: An oscillating mechanism capable of timing rhythms and likened to the pendulum of a mechanical clock (by contrast to an hour-glass timer).

Pentose phosphate pathway: It is a type of respiration. It is a metabolic pathway (also called **Phosphogluconate Pathway**, or **Hexose Monophosphate Shunt**) parallel to glycolysis that generates NADPH and pentose as well as ribose 5 phosphate. This pathway is essential for nucleic acid synthesis.

Pentose: A five carbon simple sugar

Peptide: Chain of amino acids covalently linked by peptide bonds (-CONH-).

Perception: Interaction between stimulus and receptor that starts the transduction processes.

Perennials: Plants that live for an indeterminate number of growing seasons. Most perennials arepofycarpic and flower once each year when they are sufficiently mature, but some are monocarpic (flower only once after several years and then die).

Peribacteroid membrane: The membrane which surrounds group of bacteroids in host plant cells.

Perisperm: Layer of nutritional tissue of diploid maternal origin arisen from the nucellus and often surrounding the endosperm. It is usually completely absorbed before maturation but forms the principal nutritive tissues.

Permanent Wilting Point (PWP): It is the condition of soil with respect to water content in soil. At this condition the water potential of soil is -15 bars. At this condition, the plant will show wilting. Unless, the soil is irrigated the plant will not recover.

Peroxisomes: Cell organelle with single membrane in some eukaryotes. Contains enzymes involved in glycolate metabolism or photorespiration.

P_{FR}: It is a form of phytochrome pigment which absorbs farred light and get converted to P_R form. It is physiologically active form.

pH: The negative logarithm of the hydrogen ion concentration in aqueous solution. $pH = -\log [H^+]$

Phage: A virus that infects bacteria.

Phase angle difference: Angular difference between the phase of one cycle and that of another.

Phase change: In the context of juvenility, the transition from the juvenile to the mature condition, permitting sexual reproduction.

Phase response curve: A graphic representation of the extent of phase shifts caused by treatments (perturbations) of short duration relative to one cycle and positioned at different parts of the cycle (a pulse experiment). Phase shifts are often plotted against the rhythm stage (e.g. *circadian time)* when the treatment was administered.

Phase shift: A change in the phase of one cycle relative to that of the original or previous cycle. Sometimes referred to as rephasing. If the phase is advanced in time relative to the reference cycle, the phase shift is positive (+) and involves the earlier occurrence of events within a cycle; if the phase is delayed, the phase shift is negative (–) and involves the later occurrence of events within a cycle.

Phase transition temperature: Lipids in membranes exist in one of several possible ordered structures in which the individual lipid molecules have more or less motional freedom. In a functional membrane, the lipids need to exist in a fluid state to allow rotational freedom and to be able to diffuse in the plane of the membrane. The temperature at which the lipids adopt a hexagonally parked structure, thus losing their diffusional freedoms, and enter a gel phase is known as the phase transition temperature.

Phase: Measure of timing of any instantaneous state within a cycle (e.g., peak, trough) of a rhythmic variable versus a reference (either internal or external).

Phenolics (Plant Phenolics): It is a group of secondary metabolites produced by plant systems with one or more phenolic residues; includes coumarins, lignins, flavonoids, tannins etc.

Phenology: The study of cyclic and seasonal natural phenomena, especially in relation to climate and plant and animal life.

Phenotype: The display of characteristics exhibited by an organism resulting from the expression of its genome in the existing environment.

Phenylalanine ammonia lyase (PAL): The enzyme catalyzing conversion of phenylalanine into transcinnamic acid with the elimination of one molecule of ammonia.

Pheophytin: Special form of chlorophyll-a in which central magnesium atom is replaced by two hydrogen atoms. It is the primary electron acceptor in the reaction center of PSII.

Phloem export rate: Rate of phloem translocation of a specified solute out of source organs (mg/s).

Phloem export: Rate of phloem translocation of a specified solute out of source organ. A basis for comparison such as per leaf, per area, or per plant should be specified mg/s or mol/s.

Phloem import rate: Rate of entry of a specified solute through phloem into a sink organ (mg/s).

Phloem import: Rate of entry of a specified solute through phloem into a sink organ. The rate should be expressed on a suitable basis such as per specific sink organ, or per fresh or dry mass of the sink organ. mg/s or mol/s.

Phloem loading: The process by which the products of carbon assimilation enter into the sieve elements/companion cell complex. The process may be (*a*) apoplastic as when solutes are transported across the plasma membrane of the sieve elements/ companion cell complex (*b*) symplastic as when solutes are transported from surrounding mesophyll into the sieve element/companion cell complex through symplastic connections. (*c*) symplastic and apoplastic when both pathways operated in parallel or alternatively. The process of transfer of food and energy material from leaf parts (source parts) to the sieve element/companion cell complex is called as phloem loading.

Phloem mass flux: Flux of specified solute through a unit of sieve element cross sectional area ($mg/m^2/s$).

Phloem mass: Flux of a specified solute through a unit of sieve element cross flux sectional area. ($mg/m^2/s$).

Phloem pressure gradient: The difference in turgor pressure in a file of sieve elements over a specified distance.

Phloem pressure: The difference in turgor pressure in a file of sieve elements over gradient a specified distance.

Phloem unloading: The process that bring about the net transport of water and solutes from sieve element in sink organs into the surrounding sink tissues. Passage out the sieve elements may be symplastic or apoplastic or both, depending on the nature of the sink.

Phloem: In vascular plants, phloem is the tissue that carries organic nutrients (known as photosynthates), in particular, sucrose, a sugar, to all parts of the plant where needed.

In trees, the phloem is the innermost layer of the bark, hence the name, derived from the Greek word meaning "bark".

Phobic response: Transient change of movement of motile organisms induced by a change in magnitude of a stimulus. The effective change can be an increase or decrease of the magnitude; that is, a step-up or stepdown of the stimulus. After the previous movement is resumed, its direction may have changed, but with no relation to the direction of the stimulus. In inhomoge neous fields, repeated phobic responses can result in patterns of distribution of the organisms; e.g., accumulation in a "light trap".

Phospholipid: Lipid having one or more hydrophilic phosphate group. It is the major component of cell membrane.

Phosphon D (2,4 dichlorophenyl tributyl phosphonium chloride)**:** An antigibberellin or growth retardant that inhibits GA biosynthesis.

Phosphorescence: Luminescence of substance that is caused by the absorption of radiations (such as light or electrons) and continues for a noticeable time after these radiations have stopped.

Phosphorylation: Phosphorylation is the process through which ATP is synthesized by addition of phosphate to ADP (in cells organelles like mitichondria and chloroplasts).

Photo blastic seeds: Photo blastic seeds are those whose germination is influenced by light. Seeds that are stimulated to germinate by light are called positively photo blastic. Seeds whose germination is inhibited by light are called negatively photo blastic.

Photo oxidation: Oxidation of a substance caused by the absorption of a photon.

Photoactive substance: A substance capable of a chemical or physical change in response to illumination.

Photoactive: It is the activation or control of a chemical, chemical reaction, or organism by light, as the activation of chlorophyll by sunlight during photosynthesis.

Photoassimilates: Organic compounds produced by photosynthetic carbon fixation.

Photoautotroph: Organism that derives its energy for food synthesis from light and is capable of using carbon dioxide as its principal source of carbon is called as photoautotroph.

Photobiology: The science of study of effects of light on biological organisms.

Photo-dormancy: Seeds with photo-dormancy germinate only under light conditions. Such seeds are therefore also called light sensitive. Photo dormancy is common among pioneer forest trees. It is operated by a biochemical phytochrome mechanism.

Photoheterotroph: A heterotrophic organism that uses light for energy but cannot use carbon dioxide as its sole carbon source and thus uses organic compounds from the environment.

Photoinhibition: Excess of light radiation causing inhibition of photosynthesis.

Photolyase: A blue light activated flavoenzyme which repairs UV-induced damage to microbial DNA.

Photolysis of water: Also called as Hill's Reaction. Photolysis of water is the process of splitting up of water in the presence of light. It occurs to replace the electron that is removed from the photosystem II. Water splits into protons, oxygen and electrons which makes the oxygen as by-product.

Photomorphogenesis: Any regulatory effects or changes of visible light on growth and developmental process of plant apart from photosynthesis is called as Photomorphogenesis and it is light-mediated development, where plant growth patterns respond to the light spectrum. Phytochrome and cryptochrome are the major photoreceptors involved in this process.

Photomorphogenic radiation: The radiation with wavelengths approximately ranging between 300-800 nm contributing to photomorphogenic responses (i.e., phototropism, flowering reproduction, elongation, dormancy) in relation to the relative quantum efficiency of the spectral quality in several discrete spectral regions.

Photon (unit = q; *i.e.*, one photon): A discrete physical unit of light energy. A quantum (the smallest, discrete particle) of electromagnetic energy with an energy of hc/λ. (h = Planck's constant; c = speed of light; λ = wavelength). Its energy is expressed in joules (J).

Photon fluence (Fp): The photon flow rate per unit spherical area.

Photon fluence rate: The photon fluence per unit time. The same as photon flux for normal incident radiation.

Photon flux (Ep): The photon flow rate per unit plane surface area; sometimes also called photon flux density to emphasize the unit area.

Photonegative: It is a tendency of an organism or organ moving away from light.

Photooxidation: It is the process of losing an electron from a substance or atom or molecule when exposed to light.

Photoperiod: Duration of light or day length is referred as photoperiod.

Photoperiodic response: Duration of light or daylength is called as photoperiod. The response of plants in terms of flowering to the relative lengths of light and dark is called photoperiodic response.

Photoperiodicity: The effect on the growth and reproduction of plants or animals of varying exposure to light and darkness is called as photoperiodicity.

Photoperiodism: The response of organisms to the relative lengths of day and/or night. Most responses involve changes in growth and development (*e.g.*, flowering, tuber formation, and dormancy).

Photophosphorylation: Photophosphorylation is the synthesis of ATP from ADP and inorganic phosphate in the presence of the light. Photophosphorylation takes by three ways: (1) Nonclycic Photophosphorylation, (2) Cyclic photophosphorylation and (3) Pseudo cyclic photophosphorylation.

Photopositive: It is the tendency exhibited by an organism or organ to move towards light.

Photorespiration: It is a process by which certain plants release carbon dioxide in light. Takes place in chloroplast, peroxysomes and mitochondria. 25-40% of carbondioxide fixed in photosynthesis is lost by this process.

Photoreversibility: Describing any compound or system that can exist in two forms, and can be changed from one to another by the appropriate influence of light.

Photosensitivity: Photosensitivity is the amount to which an object reacts upon receiving photons, especially visible light.

Photosynthate (Photoassimilate)**:** The product of photosynthesis such as sugars and carbohydrates.

Photosynthesis: Photosynthesis is the single-most important physico-biochemical process in the world on which the existence of life on earth depends. It is defined as "the formation of carbon containing compounds from carbon dioxide and water by illuminated green cells, water and oxygen being the by-products. This reaction is mediated by enzyme RuBiSCO.

Photosynthetic pigments: Pigments involved in absorption light for the process of photosynthesis. The different photosynthetic pigments are: (1) Chlorophylls, (2) Carotenoids, (3) Phycobilins. Chlorophylls and carotenoids are insoluble in water and phycobilins are soluble in water.

Photosynthetic rate: It is the amount of CO_2 fixed per unit leaf area per unit time in photosynthetic organism. Denoted as 'A' - μmoles $CO_2.m^{-2}.s^{-1}$

Photosynthetic surface area: It is the total leaf area of plant.

Photosynthetically active radiation (PAR): The radiation in the wavelength range of 400–700 nm. Measured as the photosynthetic photon flux (PPF), in quanta.$m^{-2}\,s^{-1}$, or mol.$m^{-2}\,s^{-1}$ or photosynthetic irradiance (PI) in Wm^{-2} for the specified waveband, $\lambda_1 - \lambda_2$ (400–700 nm).

Photosystem: A functional unit in chloroplast that harvests light energy to drive electron transport and generates proton motive force for the synthesis of ATP. There are two photosystems, photosystem I and photosystem II which involved in photosynthetic electron transport chain.

Phototropin: Product of PHOT 1 gene which has been postulated to be a blue light receptor in phototropism, chloroplast movements and stomatal opening.

Phototropism: The growth of a plant toward any stimulus is called tropism, and the growth of a plant toward a light stimulus is called phototropism-photo means light. The bending movement of stem tips towards the light source is called phototropism. Here the light provides the stimulus. The actinic part of the white light that causes the positive curvature movement is blue light. This indicates that the plant cells which respond to this light must possess a pigment system which is capable of absorbing the blue light. This pigment has been identified as riboflavin and it is called as "cryptochrome".

Phraeatophyte: A plant with the ability to thrive in a dry environment, in which high evaporative demands are met by having roots deep enough to reach a permanent water table.

Phragmoplasts: During late anaphase or early telophase in a dividing cell, at equatorial plane, fine granular structures appears, which condense to form cell plate or middle lamella.

PHY genes: The genes encoding apoprotein of the pigment phytochrome.

Phyllotaxy: Phyllotaxy is the arrangement of leaves on plant stem. There are three types of phyllotaxy. They are Alternate, Opposite, Whorled phyllotaxy.

Physical dormancy: A physical or physiological condition of viable seed, which prevents germination even in the presence of favorable conditions. Physical dormancy is caused by a hard and impermeable seed-coat or fruit enclosure which prevents imbibition and sometimes also gaseous exchange. The phenomenon is often referred to as 'hard seed', although this term is usually reserved for impermeable seeds of Leguminosae.

Physiological drought: Plant water deficit (i.e., low tissue water potential) caused by salinity, low soil water potential, or other stress factors.

Physiological dryness: Non-availability of sufficient water to plants even when they are growing in soil with plenty of water.

Phytase: The enzyme catalyzing the breakdown of phosphate rich seed storage product called phytin during seed germination.

Phytin: It is compound which acts as store for phosphate in seeds. It is the calcium, magnesium and potassium salt of phytic acid.

Phytoalexins: Phytoalexins are antimicrobial and often antioxidative substance synthesized de novo by plants that accumulate rapidly at areas of pathogen infection. They are broad spectrum inhibitors, which inhibits the growth of pathogen and are chemically diverse with different types characteristic of particular plant species.

Phytochelatins: Sulphur rich metal binding polypeptides found in plants. The general formula is $[Glu(-Cys)_nGly]$, where n = 2 to 11. Phytochelatins serve to shuttle toxic metal from cytoplasm to vacuole where they are sequestered by organic acids.

Phytochrome: Phytochrome is a photoreceptor which absorbs specifically red light and brings photomorphogenesis in plants. It exists in two forms inside the plant system as P_{red} and P_{farred} form. It is sensitive to light in the red and far-red region of the visible spectrum. The developmental process which is mediated by phytochrome are seed germination, inhibition of intermodal elongation, flower induction, etc.

Phytochromobilin: The chromophore of phytochrome.

Phytoecdysone: A group of secondary metabolites especially steroids (triterpenes) which are produced by the plant and are strong deterrents to insects because of their similarity in chemical structure to insect moulting hormones. When ingested by insect herbivores, phytoecdysones disrupt the insect's moulting cycle.

Phytoferritin: An iron protein complex found in plants.

Phytohormones (Plant growth hormone): These are organic substance produced by the plant. They are active in very minute quantities. They are synthesized in one of the parts of the plant and translocated to another part where they influence specific physiological, biochemical and morphological changes. Plant hormones also known as phytohormones eg Auxin, cytokinin, GA, ABA and Ethylene.

Phytol ($C_{20}H_{39}OH$): It is the tail region of chlorophyll pigment. Phytol is the 20 carbon isoprenoid alcohol that is esterified to the 4-pyrrole ring of the chlorophyll molecule and anchors it in the photosynthetic membranes.

Phytomining: Utilisation of plants in recovery of valuble metals. This technique involves growing of crop of metal-hyperaccumulator, which is then harvested, dried and smelted to recover the metal.

Phytoremediation: Utilising the plants to remove the contaminants from the environment.

Phytosiderophores: Iron binding ligands in higher plants.

Phytotron: It is an enclosed research green house used for studying interactions between environment and plant growth.

Phytotropins: Inhibitors of auxin transport.

Phytotoxin: It is a poisonous substance produced by plant.

Pitch length: The number of base pairs per turn of a duplex helix.

PIN 1: It is a membrane protein which facilitates the polar transport of auxins. It is situated at the basal ends of conducting cells. Look pin-shaped in immunofluorescence microscopy, hence called PIN proteins.

Plant ash: Ash is the residue of burned plant parts like bark, wood, saw dust, leaves, woody debris, pulp, husk, hulls and other plant debris.

Plant growth regulator: A compound that when applied at low concentrations (1 nM or less) modifies the growth or development of the plant. A plant growth regulator can be either an endogenous compound (*e.g.*, indole acetic acid) or a synthetic compound (*e.g.*, a-napthale acetic acid), but the term is primarily applied to synthetic compounds.

Plant growth substances: The growth of the plant is regulated through gene action and environmental conditions. There are substances which are produced by plants themselves which regulate their growth and many physiological and biochemical activities.

Plant movements : In response to various environmental factors, or by themselves plants exhibit various types of movements. Many of these movements are autonomous in nature and others are in response to external stimuli like light, soil, water, touch and chemicals. Any of the above mentioned agents which induce certain changes in the plants is referred to as stimulants. Reaction of the plant body to such stimulus is called response.

Plant Physiology: It is the study of vital phenomena in plants. It is the study of continuous natural things in plants. It is the study of the functions of cell, cell constituents, tissue, organ of plant and also it is the study of processes in plants like photosynthesis, respiration, transpiration, ion and water absorption, etc.

Plaque: Clearing of bacterial lawn caused by a virus infection initiated by a single bacteriophage.

Plaque-forming unit: (PFU) A quantitative measure of the number of viruses descended from a single colony required to clear an area of a bacterial lawn.

Plasma membrane: Membrane surrounding the cytoplasm in a cell.

Plasma membrane H+ATPase: An ATPase bound to the plasma membrane that transports H^+ across the plasma membrane.

Plasmid: DNA that can replicate independently within a bacterial cell; engineered plasmids serve as cloning vectors for the insertion of foreign DNA into a host.

Plasmodesmata: Cytoplasmic strands that traverse through pits in cell walls and connect protoplasts of adjacent cells to form the interconnected cytoplasmic unit referred as symplast.

Plasmolysis: The withdrawal of water from a plant cell causing the protoplast to contract away from the cell wall (which may shrink elastically if the cell had been under turgor).

Plasticity: The adaptability of an organism to changes in its environment or differences between its various habitats. The adaptability might be changes in morphology or changes in duration of developmental changes to survive and grow in that environment.

Plastid: Plastids are major organelles found in the cells of plants and algae. Plastids are the site of manufacture and storage of important chemical compounds used by the cell. Plastids often contain pigments used in photosynthesis, and the types of pigments present can change or determine the cell's colour.

Plastochron index: (*PI*) Indicates comparative developmental age of a shoot: , where *L* is leaf length, Lr is reference leaf length (e.g., L, = 10 mm), and *n* is serial number of the leaf just longer than Lr. Assumes leaves are growing exponentially with equal relative rates, and *plastochron* is constant.

Plastochron ratio: (a) (1) At the shoot apex, $a = rn/rn + 1$, where *rn* is the radial distance from the apex to the center of a leaf primordium *n,* and *rn* + 1, is the distance to the next younger primordium; (2) more generally, the ratio of a measured attribute of two successive leaves of a growing shoot, as, for leaf length (L), $a = Ln/Ln + 1$.

Plastochron: (1) The period of time between the commencement of two successive, repetitive processes, as between the initiations of two successive leaf primordia; (2) by extension, the time period between corresponding stages of development of two successive leaves.

Plastocyanin (PC): Plastocyanin is a copper-containing protein involved in electron-transfer. The protein is a monomer, with a molecular weight around 10,500 Daltons, and 99 amino acids in most vascular plants. It is a member of the plastocyanin family of copper-binding proteins.

Plastoquinone (PQ): An important polypeptide in photosynthetic electron transport chain that connects Cytb6/f complex to PS II. It transports both electron and H^+. It involves in vectorial translocation of protons from stoma to lumen. It is considered as a energy conserving site.

Plating: Growing bacterial colonies, transformed or otherwise, on a Petri plate.

Ploidy: The numbers of copies of a genome found in a given species; haploid has one copy; diploid, two; etc.

Plumule: The first bud (stem apex with leaves) of embryo in seed plants.

Poikilohydric: Plants that equilibrate with the water potential of their environment and, for land plants, are capable of assuming a wide range of hydration states.

Poikilotherm: An organism whose temperature varies with that of its environment.

Polar group (Hydrophilic): It is water loving group. It is soluble in water.

Polar Transport: Polar auxin transport (PAT) is the directional cell-to-cell transport of the plant hormone auxin. It results from the polar/asymmetric localisation at the plasma membrane of the auxin efflux carriers of the PIN family, which are secondary transporters that export auxin out of the cells.

Pollen tube: Pollen tube is the tubular protuberance of maturing male gametophytes in seed plants, occurring during fertilization. In angiosperms the pollen germinates on the stigma and grows through the style to reach the ovule.

Pollen vector: The vehicle by which pollen is transferred from the male flower or strobilus or the female flower or strobilus. For example: wind, water, or minerals. In animal pollinated species usually called as pollinator.

Pollen: The male gametophyte of the seed plants produced in the anther or in the strobili. Wind pollinated species have a large production of light (in coniferous usually winged) pollen. Animal pollinated species often have sticky pollen.

Pollination droplet: Pollination droplet is the droplet of fluid exuded from the micropyle of the gymnosperms at pollination, the function of which is to catch the pollen and later upon evaporation draw the pollen into the pollen chamber.

Pollination: Pollination is the process of deposition of pollen on the receptive part of the female flower. In angiosperms it is the stigma, and in gymnosperm it is the ovule tip.

Pollinator: Pollinator is the pollination agent. It is a living organism transferring pollen. For example: insects, birds, or bats.

Polyembryony: Polyembryony is the phenomenon of two or more embryos developing from a single fertilized egg (in humans, identical twins). Polyembryony occurs regularly in many plants and animals.

Polyadenylation: The post-transcriptional addition of adenylates to the 3' - end of a mRNA molecule; poly(A) refer to the presence of multiple A residues.

Polyamines: It is considered as new generation growth regulators. It is group of polyvalent cationic organic compounds containing more than one aminoacids and has a role in abiotic stress tolerance.

Polycarpic species: Plants that flower during more than one season (often many seasons); all polycarpic species are perennials. In contrast to with monocarpic species.

Polycistronic m-RNA: In prokaryotes, m-RNA with more than one cistrons, translatable to form individual proteins.

Polymerase chain reaction (PCR): A reaction in which a template of DNA is elongated by cycling of temperatures in a reaction chamber with primer(s) and all possible nucleotides in excess.

Polymerase: The enzyme by which DNA and RNA are replicated from a template.

Polynucleotide: A chain of nucleotides; DNA or RNA in which 3' hydroxyl group of pentose sugar on one nucleotide is joined to 5'-OH of pentose of next nucleotide by a phosphodiester bond.

Polyol: A compound containing many alcohol groups.

Polyomics: The platform "Polyomics" combines all relevant genome and postgenome technologies, i.e., genomics, transcriptomics, proteomics and metabolomics. It is dedicated to the genome-based development of new strains for the industrial production of biotechnologically relevant substances.

Polypeptide: A long chain of amino acids joined by peptide linkages.

Polyprotic acids: Acids that contain more than one ionisable hydronium ions per mole of the acid and ionize to give more than one H^+ ions per mole.

Polyribosome (Polysome): Complex of m-RNA molecule with two or more ribosomes actively engaged in synthesis of proteins.

Polysaccharide: A linear or branched polymer of monosaccharide units linked together by glycosidic bonds.

Polyterpene: High molecular weight terpenes containing large number isoprene residues such as rubber.

Porins: The intergral proteins present in the outer membrane of chloroplast or mitochondria which serve as large non-selective channels.

P-proteins (Phloem proteins): In sieve tube elements of phloem large amounts of proteins present lining the inner walls. They function as a puncture repair substance and plug the damage sites in sieve elements to prevent loss of food material during translocation.

Porphyrin: A complex planar structure made up of four pyrrols covalently joined into a ring and has iron at the center (as in cytochromes) and magnesium atom (as in chlorophyll).

Post-transcriptional regulation: Regulation of gene expression after the synthesis of the primary transcript, as at the level of processing or degradation of transcripts.

Post-translational regulation: Control of gene expression after translation, as at the level of processing or degradation of proteins.

Potometer: An instrument to measure the rate of transpiration.

ppm Solutions: A one ppm solution is a solution in which one milligram of a substance dissolved in 1000 mL of solvent or water.

P_R: A form of phytochrome which absorbs red light and get converted to P_{FR} form. It is stable form of phytochrome.

Prechilling (stratification): The treatment in which imbibed (moist) seeds or dormant plants are subjected to cold temperatures (usually a few degrees above freezing and preferably fluctuating) for some interval of time with the goal of breaking dormancy and promoting active growth; not to be confused with vernalization, which is a promotion of reproductive growth by cold treatment.

Precision: The ability of the instrument to consistently reproduce a value of a measured quantity.

Precocious germination: Germination of seeds without undergoing a dormancy phase, sometimes when the seed is attached to the fruit itself.

Precocious: Term applied to switching of developmental pathways prior to natural maturity, as in flowering induced chemically or germination of immature seed.

Precursor: Substance which precedes or is derived from an available source. The term "precursor" is applied to an inactive substance converted to an active one (such as an enzyme, vitamin, or hormone). The term "precursor" applies to any chemical that is transformed into another.

Premature termination: Termination of transcription before the end of the coding sequence resulting in an incomplete transcript.

Preparatory phase (utilisation phase): First half of glycolysis where glucose get converted to glyceraldehyde 3 phosphate/dihydroxy acetone phosphate in which there is utilization of two ATP occurs.

Pressure flow: As applied to phloem transport, the mass flow of water and solutes along a pressure gradient.

Pressure flow hypothesis: The theory of osmotically-driven pressure flow within the phloem; pressure builds up in the sieve element-companion cell complexes in the source as water moves into these sieve element members in response to high solute concentrations therein; pressures within the sieve element members are less in the sink regions as solutes exit from the phloem. First proposed by E. Munch in 1930.

Pressure potential (Y_p): The hydrostatic pressure exerted on the wall of a cell by water.

Primary active transport: Direct coupling of metabolic energy with carrier mediated active transport.

Primary dormancy: Primary dormancy is the term for when the seed is released from the plant already in a dormant state. This differs from secondary dormancy, when the seed becomes dormant after being released due to environmental factors.

Primary event(s): The primary cellular sensor(s) or trigger(s) that initiate(s) a series of secondary events leading eventually to the visible symptoms of such strains as chilling injury. The primary event(s) must occur at the critical stress level (e.g., critical temperature) for the species or tissue, must be rapid, and in the short term, reversible.

Primary transcript: An RNA synthesized directly from its DNA template prior to processing, polyadenylation, or editing.

Primary wall: The cell wall layer that is deposited during periods of active cell expansion.

Primer: Short, single-stranded nucleotide segment that initiates the replication of DNA from a template.

Probe: A DNA, RNA, or protein used to identify or isolate a specific target DNA, RNA, or protein.

Programmed cell Death (PCD): See apotopsis

Prokaryotes: Organism with single chromosome in the cells that is not enclosed in a membrane and also lack other membrane bound organelles. Bacteria and cyanobacteria.

Prolamellar body: A highly ordered para crystalline structure found in etioplasts.

Promoter: The region of DNA that binds RNA polymerase II to initiate transcription; promoters may be constitutive or "turned on" in response to a variety of signals.

Proplastid: Plastid develops from this small self replicating vesicular organelle.

Prosthetic group: Non protein component of a conjugated protein.

Proteasome: A large proteolytic enzyme complex in eukaryotic cells that degrades unwanted proteins with molecular mass of more than 1.5 megadaltons.

Protein: A macromolecule which is required for the growth, consisting of one or more polypeptide chains.

Protein motifs or folds: A motif is a short conserved sequence pattern associated with distinct functions of a protein. It is often associated with a distinct structural site performing a particular function.

Protein structure: primary (1° **structure).** The amino-acid sequence of a protein.

Protein structure: quarternary (4° **structure)** The organization of some proteins from multiple polypeptide subunits. Homopolymeric proteins are composed of identical subunits; heteropolymeric proteins are composed of dissimilar subunits.

Protein structure: secondary (2° **structure)** The local conformation or folding of the protein's backbone, as into helices or pleated sheets.

Protein structure: tertiary (3° **structure)** The three-dimensional organization of a protein.

Protein targeting: The process whereby proteins following synthesis are directed to specific locations in or outside the cell. This process is determined by short sequences of amino acids in the proteins called signal sequences.

Proteome: The entire complement of proteins synthesized by a cell or organisms at a given time.

Proteomics: Refers to the study of proteomes.

Protochlorophyllide: Precursor molecule of chlorophyll.

Proton-ATPase (H+ ATPase): Also known as P-type ATPase. It is electrogenic pump located in plasma membrane and tonoplast pumping protons across the membranes.

P-type ATPases are structurally distinct from F-type ATPases. They hydrolyse ATP instead of synthesizing it. ATPases of mitochondria and chloroplasts are called as F-type ATPases.

Proton motive force: Proton motive force (PMF) is the force that promotes movement of protons across membranes downhill the electrochemical potential. In most cases the proton motive force is generated by an electron transport chain which acts as a proton pump, using the energy of electrons from an electron carrier (Gibbs free energy of redox reactions) to pump protons (hydrogen ions) out across the membrane, separating the charge across the membrane.

Protoplasm: It refers to the entire contents of living cell : cytoplasm with nucleus.

Protoplast: Entire contents of a living cell enclosed by plasma membrane after removal of the Cell wall.

Protoplast fusion: Somatic fusion, also called protoplast fusion, is a type of genetic modification in plants by which two distinct species of plants are fused together to form a new hybrid plant with the characteristics of both, a somatic hybrid.

Pseudocyclic photophosphorylation: Another type of light-induced phosphorylation of ADP called pseudocyclic photophosphorylation occurs when reduced ferredoxin transfers electrons through a series of reactions to O_2 (not to $NADP^+$ or P_{700}), with the result that water and ATP are formed.

Pseudogenes: A gene rendered non-functional by addition or deletion to its structure; probably related to duplicated genes.

Pteridene: A nitrogen containing compound with two six membered rings; component of riboflavin.

PTOX (Plastid terminal oxidase):Enzyme present in thylakoid membranes. It oxidises plastoquinol and reduces oxygen to water during chlororespiration. Very similar to alternate oxidase (AOX) found in mitochondria.

Pulsed-field electrophoresis: The separation of genomic, or very large DNAs in a semi-solid medium by electric pulses rather than constant current.

Pumping activity: Forces responsible for ascent of sap are developed in medullary rays and xylem parenchyma due to the periodic changes in permeability of these cells. These periodic changes in osmotic pressure is called as pumping activity.

Pumps: Proteins present on the membrane, which facilitate active transport of ions such as H^+ and Ca^{++} across the biological membrane.

Purines: Nitrogenous base found in nucleic acids. Adenine and guanine.

Puromycin: An antibiotic that inhibits protein synthesis specifically and reversibly by preventing the elongation of growing polypeptide chain.

Pyranose: Simple sugar having six membered pyran ring structure.

Pyrethroids: Monoterpene esters with strong insecticidal properties in some plants such as chrysanthemum.

Pyridoxal phosphate (Vitamin B_6): A coenzyme that acts as carrier of amino group in transamination reactions.

Pyrimidine: Nitrogenous base present in nucleic acids. Cytosine, thymine and uracil.

Pyrophosphate(PPi): Molecule which has two phosphates in anhydride linkages.

Pyruvate dehydrogenase: A multienzyme complex present in mitochondria that catalyses oxidative decarboxylation of pyruvic acid to acetyl CoA, CO_2 and NADH.

Q

Q_{10} (Temperature coefficient): The ratio of the rate of chemical reaction at a particular temperature to the rate of that chemical reaction exactly at 10°C lower.

Qualitative photoperiod: Qualitative plants are those in which a particular photoperiod is an absolute requirement for the occurrence of a response. Ex: Common cocklebur

Qualitative response (absolute response, obligatory response): A plant response, usually flowering, that absolutely depends on some day length, temperature, or other environmental stimulus. If the plant does not experience the required stimulus, the response does not occur (*e.g.*, the plant remains vegetative). Opposite to quantitative response.

Quantasomes : Quantasomes are particles found in the thylakoid membrane of chloroplasts in which photosynthesis takes place. They are embedded in a para crystalline array on the surface of thylakoid discs in chloroplasts. They are composed of lipids and proteins that include various photosynthetic pigments and redox carriers.

Quantitative photoperiod: Quantitative photoperiod plants are those in which a particular photoperiod is not an absolute requirement for the occurrence of a response. The response will occur even in the absence of absolute requirement, but there will be early or late response depending upon the changes in the requirement conditions.

Quantitative response (facultative response): A plant response that is changed in number or developmental rate (e.g., more flowers or tubers) by a treatment such as a particular day length or an exposure to a period of low temperatures. Opposite to a qualitative or absolute response. In the absence of the treatment, the response still occurs but at a much slower rate or fewer organs are produced.

Quantum requirement: Quantum Requirement is the number of photons required to release one molecule of oxygen in the photosynthesis.

Quantum yield: Number of oxygen molecule released per photon of light in photosynthesis is called as Quantum Yield.

Quantum: Energy contained in a photon.

Quenching: Dissipation of energy stored in light excited chlorophyll molecules.

Quiscent centre: A small region in the centre of the root apical meristem just behind the root cap where cell divisions proceed very slowly or not at all. However, the cells in this region are capable of resuming meristematic activity in case the tissue surrounding them is damaged.

Quiscent seeds: The seeds that germinate readily when placed in suitable environmental conditions necessary for seed germination.

Quiescence: Quiescence is a state of quietness or inactivity.

R

Radiant energy (Q_e, J): The transfer of energy of radiation.

Radiation frost: Heat radiated from surface of soil, trees, and any other solid particles to reduce the temperature low enough to cause frost conditions. Solid particles lose heat more rapidly than air, reducing the surface temperature. Eventually the air at low levels becomes cool and heavy compared to air at higher elevations. Occurs more readily on cloudless nights when there is no barrier for retaining the heat (i.e., a barrier that radiates the heat back to earth).

Radiation: The emission and propagation of electromagnetic waves or particles through space or matter.

Radical (Free Radical): An atom or a group of atoms with an unpaired electron which can exist independently for short period during the course of chemical reaction.

Radicle: Embryonic root of seed plants.

Random-amplifled-polymorphic DNA (RAPD): The amplification of sequences of DNA distributed randomly throughout a genome by PCR technology to analyse genetic structure or relatedness of populations.

Randomization: The assignment of treatments to experimental units at random. This is done to obtain unbiased estimates of the treatment effects and mean square error. It removes personal bias or even the appearance of such bias.

Randomized Block Design (RBD): The experimental units are grouped or blocked in such a way that the variability from block to block is greater than the variability within blocks. Each treatment occurs once in each block.

Raphe: Ridge on seed coat formed from *adnate funiculus*.

Reaction center: The chlorophyll along with associated proteins and redox carriers which are directly involved in light driven redox reactions of photosynthesis.

Reactive oxygen species: Whenever oxygen species has extra electron or more energy, then they will be reactive and hence they are called as reactive oxygen species. Reactive oxygen species or free radicals of oxygen in plants are singlet oxygen, superoxide, hydrogen peroxide and hydroxyl radicals. Electron transport chains are major sites of premature electron leakage to oxygen generating superoxide. Oxygen species creates oxidative stress at cellular level.

Reading frame: A specific mode of reading codon triplets to produce a functional polypeptide.

Recalcitrant seeds: Seeds that have a very limited storage period that usually cannot be extended by dry and cold conditions. They are generally large and frequently are tropical species; they germinate at once after ripening.

Receptor: Recipient of a signal, such as a hormone, protein, light, etc., that binds to a specific site and initiates a reaction.

Reciprocity: The response depends quantitatively neither on the intensity of the stimulus alone, nor on its duration, but on the product of both parameters. If reciprocity holds, this is usually taken as a lack of rate-limiting processes in the transduction chain or in recovery processes of the receptor.

Reclamation: With reference to saline soils, the process of removing excess salt to a level that permits production of plants without significant adverse effects.

Recombinant: An organism whose genetic makeup is altered by the stable insertion of a foreign DNA.

Red drop : Sharp decrease in quantum yield of photosynthesis by using only monochromatic light of wavelengths greater than 680 nm in red part of spectrum.

Redifferentiation: Cells produced by dedifferentiation tissues again loose back their capacity to divide and mature to perform specific function is called redifferentiation.

Redox couple: An electron donor and its oxidized form (NADH and NAD^+).

Redox potential (E_0'): The potential required in a cell to produce oxidation at anode and reduction at cathode. It is determined at particular temperature and pH usually 250°C and pH 7 and is expressed in terms of volts (V). A redox system with a high negative E_0' value acts as electron donor and the one with comparatively less negative or high positive E_0' value acts as electron acceptor.

Reducing sugar: A sugar molecule in which atleast one function group is open and not involved in glycosidic bond formation.

Reduction: Addition of electron to a substance or compound or molecule is called as reduction. Calvin cycle has a reduction step that leads to the formation of trioses. The step involves utilisation of 2 molecules of NADPH for reduction and 2 molecules of ATP for phosphorylation.

Reductive amination: Reductive amination (also known as reductive alkylation) is a form of amination that involves the conversion of a carbonyl group to an amine via an intermediate amine. The carbonyl group is most commonly a ketone or an aldehyde.

Reductive carboxylic acid cycle: A biochemical pathway operative in some photosynthetic bacteria for carbon assimilation. Each turn of this cycle incorporates four molecules of carbondioxide and results in net synthesis of one oxaloacetic acid molecule. This further metabolized to provide C_2 – C_6 carbon compounds that are utilized for synthesis of variety of organic compounds in bacterial cells.

Reductive pentose phosphate cycle (RPP cycle) : Another name for Calvin cycle.

Regrowth: The ultimate viability test to determine survival following a stress. Plants or cells are grown for a given period of time following a stress and then evaluated for either root and shoot regeneration or increase in mass.

Rejuvenation: Reversion (usually only partial) of mature woody plants to a secondary juvenile phase by such treatments as pruning, grafting, and treatment with gibberellins.

Relative Growth Rate (RGR): The term was coined by Williams (1946). Relative Growth Rate (RGR) expresses the total plant dry weight increase in a time interval in relation to the initial weight. Expressed as unit dry weight / unit dry weight / unit time (mg $g^{-1}day^{-1}$).

Relative humidity: Relative humidity (RH) is the ratio of partial pressure of water vapour to the equilibrium vapour pressure of water at the same temperature. Relative humidity depends on temperature and the pressure of the system of interest.

Relative plastochron growth rate: Relative growth rate of leaves or leaf primordia, regarding time as measured in plastochrons.

Relative water content: Relative water content is the measure of plant water status. RWC is the water content of a given amount of leaf relative to its fully hydrated or fully turgid state.

Repair: The process by which the stress-induced injury of a plant is partially or completely reversed following removal of the stress.

Reporter gene: The coding region of a surrogate gene whose product is easily observed, *e.g.*, CAT, GUS, LacZ, fused to the promoter of a native gene whose product is difficult to detect. Demonstration of the surrogate gene analyzes the native gene: its function, localization, and responses to developmental and environmental signals.

Repressor: Negative regulation of a gene in response to an external factor; e.g., decreased expression of the gene encoding nitrate reductase in response to ammonium.

Resonance transfer: The transfer of energy form molecule to molecule from one excited molecule to another.

Respiration : It is a process of oxidation of organic compounds to carbondioxide and water during which energy is released which will be useful for maintenance and growth of tissues.

Respiratory balance sheet: It is process of calculation of the net gain of ATP for every glucose molecule oxidised.

Respiratory Quotient (RQ): Respiratory quotient is the ratio of the volume of carbon dioxide produced to the volume of oxygen consumed in respiration over a period of time. Its value can be one, zero, more than 1 or less than one. It is a dimensionless number used in calculation of basal metabolic rate. RQ calculated as follows:

RQ = Volume of CO_2 evolved/Volume of O_2 absorbed

Respiratory substrate: A respiratory substrate is a molecule from which energy can be liberated to produce ATP in a living cell. Glucose is not the only respiratory substrate. All carbohydrates, lipids and proteins can also be used as respiratory substrates.

Restriction enzyme: An enzyme, usually of bacterial origin, that cuts DNA at specific base pairs, producing restriction fragments.

Restriction-fragment-length polymorphism (RFLP): Characterization of a genome by comparison of sizes of selected restriction fragments.

Revernalization: Effective chilling treatment of plants that have been devernalized.

Reverse stomatal rhythym: Nocturnal opening and closing of stomata in CAM plants.

Rheotropism: Movement of curvature in which a plant organ *i.e.*, roots, turn away from water current. The tendency of some plants to respond to a current of water by growing with it (Positive rheotaxis) or against it (Negative rheotaxis).

Rhizobia: Group of nitrogen fixing bacteria.

Rhizogenesis: The development of root from the callus is called rhizogenesis.

Rhizosphere: The soil around the root.

Rhythm splitting: The subdivision of rhythmic processes into two or more groups with similar or different periods, sometimes observed in organisms under free-running conditions.

Ri plasmid: Plasmid of Agrobacterium rhizogenes; plasmid confers "hairy-root" pathogenicity to Agrobacterium species.

Ribonucleic acid (RNA): A polynucleotide in which the sugar is ribose rather than deoxyribose; the molecule of which messenger, ribosomal, and transfer RNAs, and some viral genomes are composed.

Riboflavin (Vitamin B_2 or G): Important constituent of FMN and FAD.

Ribose: A 5 carbon simple sugar

Ribosomal RNA (r-RNA): RNA components of ribosome.

Ribosomes: Cell organelle where protein synthesis takes place.

Ribozymes: An enzyme which is not a protein. RNA molecule with catalytic properties.

Rieske-protein: Component of photosynthetic electron transport chain. It is a iron sulphur protein.

Ripeness-to-flower: A little understood condition of a plant that is reached at a certain age when it is capable of becoming induced to flower in response to a photoperiodic or other (e.g., temperature) treatment.

Ripening: Ripening is a process in fruits that causes them to become more palatable. In general, a fruit becomes sweeter, less green, and softer as it ripens. Even though the acidity of fruit increases as it ripens, the higher acidity level does not make the fruit seem tarter. This is attributed to the Brix-Acid Ratio.

RNA (Ribonucleic acid): A polynucleotide where pentose sugar is ribose.

RNA editing: The substitution, addition or removal of bases in a transcript to produce a "correct" transcript.

RNA polymerase: An enzyme that catalyses the formation of RNA from ribonucleotide triphosphates, using DNA as a template.

Root cap: A mass of cells covering the apex of growing point of root and protects it from mechanical damage when root pierces through the soil.

Root initiation: Stem cutting of some plants readily form adventitious roots when put in the soil. Rooting is promoted by the auxin produced in buds and leaves.

Root pressure: It is defined as a pressure developed in the xylem vessels as a result of the metabolic activities of roots. Root pressure is developed, when rate of water absorption is more than the transpiration and as a result of which water is pushed up in tracheary elements of roots.

Rosette plant: A plant with leaves coming from a greatly shortened stem at ground level; typical of many biennials during the first year (*e.g.*, beets).

Rotenone: Isoflavonoid with strong insecticidal properties. Specifically inhibit electron flow from Fe-S protein in complex I to Ubiquinone (UQ).

Rough Endoplasmic reticulum: Endoplasmic reticulum associated with ribosomes.

Rubber: A natural product produced in latex of over 300 genera of angiosperms. It is high molecular weight polyisoprene or polyterpene compound consisting of large number of isopentenyl units in which C-C bond have cis configuration.

RuBisCO (Ribulose bisphosphate carboxylase/Oxygenase): It is world's most abundant enzyme. Found in the stroma of chloroplast of plants. Rate limiting enzyme in photosynthetic reaction. Bifunctional enzyme which can add carbondioxide to RuBP (Carboxylation) and add oxygen to RuBP (Oxygenation).

RuBP (Ribulose bisphosphate): A five carbon ketopentose sugar. It is the initial acceptor of carbondioxide in Calvin cycle.

Running (running phase): Locomotion of peritrichous bacteria (having a uniform distribution of flagella over the body surface; movement more or less straight forward), usually caused by counterclockwise rotation of flagella.

S

Salicyclic acid: Salicyclic acid (from Latin salix, willow tree, from the substances used to be obtained) is aminohydroxybenzoic acid, a type of phenolic acid and a beta hydracid. It has the formula $C_7H_6O_3$. This colourless crystalline organic acid is widely used in organic synthesis and function as a plant hormone. It is derived from the metabolic of salicin. In addition to being an important active metabolic of aspirin (acetylsalicyclic acid), which acts in part as a prodrug to salicyclic acid, it is probably best known for its use as a key ingredient in topical anti-acne products. The salts and esters of salicyclic acid are known as salicylates.

Salination: The process of accumulation of soluble salts in the soil.

Saline adaptation: Genetic modification of individuals in a population that increases their ability to survive excess salt.

Saline adjustment: Physiological and biochemical changes of individual plants that increase their ability to survive excess salt.

Saline soil: A soil that has an electrical conductivity in a saturated-paste extract greater than 4 dS/m. The soluble salt content of such soils is sufficient to interfere with the growth of many plant species. Sensitive crop plants are affected at half this salinity and highly tolerant ones at about twice this salinity.

Saline stress: External salt concentrations sufficiently high to reduce plant growth. Injury may result from osmotic stress, ion toxicities (see ionic effect), and/or nutritional imbalance.

Saline-sodic soil: A soil that is both saline and sodic.

Salinity stress: Excess total soluble salts in soil or in water creates stress is called salinity stress. Salts become toxic to plants in high concentration.

Salinity threshold: The maximum salinity a plant can tolerate without a reduction in growth.

Salinity: Presence of inorganic ions in solution. The term often is used to refer to ion levels high enough to cause osmotic stress. The predominant ions include Na^+, Ca^{2+}, Mg^{2+} , Cl^-, SO_4^{2-}, and HCO_3^-. These ions may have specific ion effects as well as osmotic effects.

Salt glands: Specialized cells or groups of cells on or near the surface of leaves or stems that secrete salt and help control levels of salt in plant cells.

Salt resistance: The ability of plants to take some action or employ some mechanism to avoid detrimental effects of salinity. The mechanism of resistance should be specified if it is known.

Salt respiration: The rate of respiration, which is solely due to anion absorption, is called anion respiration or salt respiration.

Salt tolerance: The ability of plants to cope with salinity.

Salt-affected soil: A soil containing excessive concentrations of soluble salts and/or exchangeable sodium.

Salt balance: A steady-state concentration of salt determined by a balance between the influx of salt and the efflux of salt from the system. This balance is frequently disturbed by inappropriate management of water and/or soils or a change in the climatic conditions.

Salvage pathway: Recycling pathway for the synthesis of biomolecule from an intermediate of the degradative pathway for that molecule. Opposite to *de novo* synthesis.

SAM (s-adenosyl methionine or AdoMet): Intermediate in ethylene biosynthesis pathway.

Saponification: Alkaline hydrolysis of acylglycerols to produce salts of fatty acids.

Sample Size: The number of experimental units used in each treatment of an experiment.

Sand Culture: Growing of plants in pure quartz sand to investigate their nutritional needs, growth, and development under laboratory conditions is called as sand culture.

SAR (systemic acquired resistance): When any pathogen attacks the plant, the plant will develop resistance throughout the plant body against pathogens and arrest the further infection. This is called as systemic acquired resistance.

Saturated condition: When the soil pores are completely filled with water then it is called as saturated condition.

Saturated lipids: Saturated lipids have single bond between carbon.

Saturated soil paste: A particular mixture of soil and water. At saturation, the soil paste glistens as it reflects light, flows slightly when the container is tipped, and the paste slides freely and cleanly from a spatula.

Saturation extract: The solution extracted from a soil at its saturation water content.

Saturation percentage: The water content of a saturated soil paste, expressed on a dry-mass percentage basis.

Scaffold proteins: Non enzymatic proteins which nucleate formation of multienzyme complexes by providing two or more specific binding sites for those proteins.

Scarification: Breaking of the seed coat barrier by mechanical treatment such as abrasion by sand or gravel or microbial action; allows penetration of water and oxygen and thus allows germination.

SCF complex (E_3 enzyme complex): It is a multiprotein enzyme complex that is involved in ubiquitination pathway of protein degradation. It is named for its first three subunits Skp1, Cullin, and F-box protein. Fourth subunit, RBX1 was also identified in this complex.

Scion: The detached plant part that is grafted to a stock.

Scoto-: Induction by darkness.

Scutellum: Single cotyledon of grass embryo.

Second messenger: A small molecule within a cell that relays a chemical message from outside the cell, as cyclic AMP.

Secondary dormancy: Secondary dormancy occurs in some non-dormant and post dormant seeds that are exposed to conditions that are not favorable for germination, like high temperatures. It is caused by conditions that occur after the seed has been dispersed. The mechanisms of secondary dormancy are not yet fully understood but might involve the loss of sensitivity in receptors in the plasma membrane.

Secondary event(s): The metabolic and cellular changes following (directly or indirectly) as consequences of the primary event and that lead to the visible symptoms of stress-induced injury. The secondary events are both time and stress-dependent. In the short term the changes induced are reversible if the stress is removed. However, if the stress is maintained, the tissue becomes unable to recover.

Secondary metabolites: These group of organic compounds such as alkaloids, terpenes, tannins, flavonoids found in plants helps them in defense against microbial pathogens, insects and other herbivores and also act as attractants for pollination and seed dispersal. They are not the products of primary metabolism, which helps in growth and development of plants.

Secondary structure: See protein structure (secondary structure)

Secondary wall: Inner most layer of cell wall which are deposited after the expansion of cell has stopped.

Second messenger: Diffusible molecule synthesized inside the cell, in response to an external signal like hormones. Examples are cAMP, cGMP, Ca^{2+}, IP_3 or diacylglycerol.

Seed coating: In coating, seeds are covered with the substance with or without an adhesive applied to the seed-coat. The coating does not significantly increase seed size or weight.

Seed dormancy: Seed dormancy refers to a state in which viable seeds fail to germinate when provided with conditions normally favourable to germination i.e. adequate moisture, appropriate temperature regime, a normal atmosphere and in some cases light. Seed dormancy is defined as a state in which seeds are prevented from germinating even under environmental conditions normally favorable for germination. These conditions are a complex combination of water, light, temperature, gasses, mechanical restrictions, seed coats, and hormone structures.

Seed germination: Germination is the process by which a plant grows from a seed. The most common example of germination is the sprouting of a seedling from a seed of an angiosperm or gymnosperm. In addition, the growth of a sporeling from a spore, such as the spores of hyphae from fungal spores, is also germination. It is the protrusion of radicle from seed coat under favourable conditions.

Seed maturation: Plants, as sessile life forms, have evolved diverse mechanisms to circumvent unfavourable growth conditions, among them interruption of the life cycle is one of the most successful strategies. During seed formation, embryo development can proceed through a maturation phase that allows the entry into a quiescent state and represents an evolutionary advantage, since it facilitates dispersal and resuming of growth under optimal environmental conditions. In the maturation phase different gene expression programmes devoted to the accumulation of storage compounds, acquisition of desiccation tolerance and entry into quiescence occur, which are highly coordinated and under fine regulatory control.

Seed viability: It is the ability of the seed to germinate under favourable conditions. Even seed will be viable under dormant condition.

Seed vigour: Seed vigour is defined as "the sum total of those properties of the seed which determine the level of activity and performance of the seed or seed lot during germination and seedling emergence".

Seed: Seeds are the dispersal and propagation units of the Spermatophyta (seed plants): Gymnosperms (conifers and related clades) and Angiosperms (flowering plants). Seeds are mature, fertilized ovules.

Seismo-: Induction by vibration (*e.g.*, by wind action, shaking, usually also by sudden contact with a solid body or a fluid).

Selectable marker: A trait whose presence or absence enables one to grow colonies or organisms with or without a specific essential component; *e.g.*, antibiotic-resistant mutants in the presence of that antibiotic, or in the absence of an otherwise essential nutrient.

Selection: Identification of a specific trait useful in singling out a transformant.

Selective amplification of microsatellite polymorphic loci (SAMPL): A PCR technique used in genome mapping.

Semiconservative replication: Duplication of DNA in which the daughter duplex contains one new and one old strand.

Semipermeable membrane: All biological membrane are semi permeable membrane. This membrane does not allow everything to pass through it. It will have restriction in solute to pass through it.

Semidian rhythm: Biological rhythm with a period of about 12 h. (The term, circasemidian, also appears in the literature to indicate a period of 12 ± 2 hours.)

Senescence: Plant senescence is the process of aging in plants. The term senescence is derived from a Latin word "Senesce" which means to grow old'. The terms Senescence, Programmed Cell Death (PCD)', Apoptosis' and Ageing' are often used synonymously in plant or animal systems. All these terms generally refer to death of cells, organs or organisms.

Sensitivity to chilling: The term used to distinguish relative sensitivity (among chilling-sensitive plant species) on the basis of their critical temperature and critical time to develop chilling injury.

Sequence: A specific string of bases in a protein or polynucleotide. As a verb, to sequence means to determine the sequences of amino acids in a protein or bases in a polynucleotide.

Sesquiterpenes: Sesquiterpenoids are defined as the group of 15 carbon compounds derived by the assembly of three isoprenoid units and they are found mainly in higher plants but also in an invertebrates. Sesquiterpenes, with monoterpenes, are an important constituent of essential oils in plants. They are the diverse group of isoprenoids. In plants they function as pheromones and juvenile hormone.

Sex expression: It is the ability of a flower in a plant to become male or female flower.

Shikimic acid pathway: This pathway is the connecting link between primary and secondary metabolism in plants. In this pathway, simple carbohydrate precursors gets converted into aromatic amino acids and phenolic compounds.

Short day plants: The short day plants, on the other hand describes plants that begin flowering when the days are shorter than critical day length. e.g., Chrysanthemum, poinsettias, Easter lily.

Short distance transport: Transportation of photosynthates over a distance of only 2-3 cells in phloem loading and phloem unloading.

Short-long-day plant (SLDP): A plant that responds photoperiodically (flowering is usually the response) to a sequence of short days followed by long days.

SI system: is a so-called coherent unit system, in which the equations between numerical values have exactly the same form (including the numerical factors) as the corresponding equations between the quantities. This is achieved by defining units for the base quantities (the base units), and then deriving further units from these base units based upon the equations between the quantities.

Sieve elements/companion cell complex: Cellular complex interconnected by specialized unilaterally branched plasmodesmata; the complex acts as an integrated physiological unit in photoassimilate transport.

Sieve tube: A series of sieve cells which lie end to end, forming a tube. Characteristic element of phloem functioning in translocation of food material synthesized within the plant.

Sigmoidal curve: When growth rate of plant organ or plant plotted against time, sigmoidal curve is obtained.

Sign Test: A test for the median of a population. It classifies each observation as being either above (+) or below (-) the hypothesized median and then tests to see if the observed proportion above the median, *P*, differs from 0.5 by using either standard binomial tables or the normal approximation to the binomial.

Signal sequence, signal peptide: A portion, usually the N-terminus, of a protein that is recognized and removed co-translationally by the endoplasmic reticulum (ER) prior to transport of the protein into the lumen of the ER.

Signal transduction: The process by which the perception of an external signal induces a result: the expression of a gene or set of genes; *e.g.*, the steps between the absorption of light by phytochrome and the synthesis of proteins of the light harvesting complex.

Signal transmission: Part of the transduction processes bridging the location of perception and that of response if they do not occur at the same sites (structures, compartments, cells, organs).

Simple diffusion: It occurs when non polar molecules like oxygen, NH_3, follow a concentration gradient moving passively through a cell lipid bilayer membrane without use of transport proteins.

Simple linear regression: A procedure for relating two continuous variables when one variable (dependent variable) is expressed as a linear function of the other (independent variable). A common use is to predict one variable based on the information provided by the other. The form of the equation is where *Y* represents the predicted value.

Sink: Any organ or part in a plant which does not have the capacity to do photosynthesis. Moreover, it is a region in which there is net efflux of solutes and water from sieve elements resulting in import into them.

Sinusoidal rhythm: A rhythm that, when the observed measurements are plotted as a function of time, exhibits a curve that approximates a sine curve.

Skeleton photoperiod: A synchronizing light:dark cycle with short light spans marking the beginning and the end of the usual light span of a 24 h cycle.

Skotomorphogenesis: Skotos means dark. Development changes of seedlings when it is grown under dark condition.

Sodic soil: A soil that has an exchangeable sodium percentage (ESP) greater than 15. The exchangeable sodium of such soils often adversely affects soil structure and may be deleterious to plant growth.

Sodicity: Presence of excess sodium in soils with a pH range of 8.5 to 10.0.

Sodium adsorption ratio (SAR): A relation between soluble sodium and soluble divalent cations that can be used to predict exchangeable sodium percentage of soil equilibrated with a given solution.

Sodium dodecyl sulfate (SDS): A detergent used to separate polymeric, or apoproteins into their monomeric subunits.

Solar tracking: In a plant when the leaf blades moves throughout the day, in such a way that solar radiation fall perpendicular to the blades is called as solar tracking. It is mediated by cryptochrome, a blue light receptor.

Solute potential: If some solutes are dissolved in pure water, the solution has fewer free water molecules and the concentration of water decreases, reducing its water potential. Hence, all solutions have a lower water potential than pure water, magnitude of this lowering due to dissolution of a solute is called solute potential. Solute potential is always negative.

Solute: The substance which is dissolved in a solution is called solute. This is referred as dispersed phase in a solution.

Solution: It is a mixture of solute with solvent. A liquid mixture in which minor component (solute) mixed with major component (solvent).

Solution culture: Refer Hydroponics

Solvent: It is substance which dissolves the solute into it in a solution. This is referred as dispersed phase of a solution.

Sorbitol: Sugar alcohol with molecular formula $C_6H_{14}O_6$. It is an osmoregulant, which gives drought tolerance to plants. It is also known as glucitol and used as sweetner.

Soret band: In spectroscopy, a Soret peak or Soret band is an intense peak in the blue wavelength region of the visible spectrum. The peak is named after its discoverer, Jacques-Louis Soret. Sometimes chlorophyll pigment has such pattern.

Source: Source is an organ which has the capacity to do photosynthesis. Moreover it is the region in which net flux of solute into elements is sufficient to cause net export from them.

Southern blot: Transfer of DNA that has been separated by electrophoresis to a membrane in order to probe it by hybridization; after E.M. Southern. In recognition of Southern's contribution, subsequent researchers named RNA or protein blots after directions also.

SPAC: The concept of transpirational water flow through a Soil-Plant-Atmosphere Continuum, usually in terms of an Ohms-Law analogy with A T as the potential gradient, transpiration as the flux, and the hydraulic resistance between any two points of the pathway as the ratio gradient/flux.

Specific Leaf Area (SLA): Specific leaf area is a measure of the leaf area of the plant to leaf dry weight and expressed in cm^2g^{-1} as proposed by Kvet *et al.*, (1971). Hence, if the SLA is high, the photosynthesizing surface will be high. However no relationship with yield could be expected.

$$SLA = Leaf\ area / Leaf\ weight$$

Specific Leaf Weight (SLW): It is a measure of leaf weight per unit leaf area. Hence, it is a ratio expressed as g cm^{-2} and the term was suggested by Pearce *et al.* (1968). More SLW/unit leaf area indicates more biomass and a positive relationship with yield can be expected.

$$SLW = Leaf\ weight / Leaf\ area$$

Specific heat: The amount of heat in joules/calories required to raise the temperature of substance by 1°C.

Specific rotation: The rotation, in degrees of the plane of plane-polarised light by a optically active compound at 25°C, with a specified concentration and path of light.

Spectral distribution: A functional or graphic expression of the relation between the spectral energy flux, spectral photon flux, or fluence rate per unit wavelength, and wavelength.

Spectral energy flow rate (e_y): The radiant energy flow rate per unit wavelength interval at wavelength λ.

Spectral energy fluence (F_{ei}): The energy fluence per unit wavelength interval at wavelength λ.

Spectral energy fluence rate: The radiant energy fluence rate per unit wavelength interval at wavelength λ.

Spectral energy flux (E_e): The radiant energy flow rate per unit plane surface per unit wavelength interval at wavelength λ.

Spectral photon fluence rate: The photon fluence rate per unit wavelength interval at wavelength λ.

Spectral photon flux: The photon flux per unit wavelength interval at wavelength A.

Spliceosome: A complex of macromolecules that removes introns and joins exons during RNA processing.

Splicing: The joining of exons into a mature mRNA.

Split gene: A gene interrupted by an intron, or non-coding sequence.

Spongy parenchyma: Spongy parenchyma lies below the palisade parenchyma. Spongy cells are irregularly shaped. These cells are very loosely arranged with numerous airspaces. As compared to palisade cells, the spongy cells contain lesser number of chloroplasts. Spongy cells facilitate the exchange of gases with the help of air spaces. The air space that is found next to the stoma is called respiratory cavity or sub-stomatal cavity.

Standard deviation (S): Approximately the average distance from the mean for a set of observations.

Standard error of estimate: The square root of the residual (or unexplained) variance in a regression model.

Standard error of the difference between two means: The difference between two means has a variance that is the sum of the variances of the individual means if the two means are independent. The standard error of this difference is the square root of the variance.

Standard error of the mean (SX): Since the mean is itself a variable, it also has standard deviation. This is denoted as and is called the standard error of the mean.

Standard error of the slope: A measure of the variability of the slope of the regression line. It has the same relationship to the slope as the standard deviation has to the original variable, *X*.

Standard free energy change (DG°): Free energy change for a reaction occurring under condition of temperature, 298 K; pressure 101.3 K Pa and all reactants and products at a unit concentration (1 M).

Standard solution: It is the solution for which the concentration is known. In analytical chemistry, a standard solution is a solution containing a precisely known concentration of an element or a substance. A known weight of solute is dissolved to make a specific volume. Standard solutions are used to determine the concentrations of other substances, such as solutions in titrations.

Starch: A complex polysaccharide act as storage polysaccharide with amylose and amylopectin component.

Statocysts: Special plant cells which contain statoliths and can sense gravity stimulus.

Statoliths: Cellular structure found in statocysts such as amyloplasts which can sense gravity stimulus and sediment at the base of the cell.

Steady growth: As in a root, growth in which the pattern of cell production and enlargement is invarient with time.

Step-up, step-down: Denotes in which direction the magnitude of the stimulus has to be changed in order to induce a phobic response or a growth response.

Stereoisomers: Isomers which are non-superimposable mirror image of each other.

Steroids: A class of lipids containing the steroid nucleus that consists of a cyclopentane ring fused to a substituted phenanthrene ring.

Stilbenes: A phenyl propanoid derivative having antifungal properties.

Stimulus (signal, input signal): A physical or chemical factor that, when interacting with the organism or cell, can elicit a movement or modify an already existing movement. Its quantity is characterized by its intensity and its duration. It can act in a scalar or in a vectorial way. A stimulus regulates the movement but does not provide the energy for it. Thus, if such a factor also provides energy for the movement, one can debate whether it should be called a stimulus (e.g., photokinesis in cyanobacteria, desmids, etc.).

Stock: The root or rooted plant to which a detached plant part (the scion*)* is grafted.

Stoichiometry: Is the branch of chemistry which involves the quantitative relationship between two or more substances especially in processes involving physical or chemical change.

Stoma (plural stomata): Leaf opening or pore in the epidermal layer of leaf cells guarded by guard cells by which gas exchange takes place.

Stomatal complex: Group of cells comprising of guard cells, subsidiary cells encompassing stomatal pore.

Stomatal closure: When the guard cells of stomata becomes flaccid, this response occurs. Plants try to close the stomata to reduce transpiration.

Stomatal density: Number of stomata per unit mm^2 of leaf surface.

Stomatal conductance: Stomatal conductance is the ease with which carbondioxide or gas moves into the stomata.

Stomatal index: It is the ratio of number of stomata to the total number of cells on the leaf epidermis (epidermal cells+guard cells) multiplied by 100.

Stomatal movement: Opening and closing movement of stomata when guard cells are turgid and flaccid respectively is called as stomatal movement.

Stomatal pore: It is a pore, found in a epidermis of leaves, stem and other organs that is used to control gas exchange. The pore is bordered by a pair of specialized epidermal cells known as guard cells.

Stomatal resistance: It is the inverse of stomatal conductance. It is the resistance offered by stomata for the entry of gases inside and outside the leaves.

Stomatal transpiration: Loss of water in form of water vapour (transpiration) through stomata is called stomatal transpiration. A large quantity of water is lost through the stomata during transpiration.

Stop codon: A codon that causes termination of transcription; specifically UAA, UAG, and UGA

Strain: The observed (deleterious) biological changes that occur in response to stress. (The terms stress and strain can be used in a manner analogous to their use in physics: stress is the force applied to an object, as a metal bar; strain is the actual change in shape of the object, as bending of the bar.)

Stratification: A process of breaking seed dormancy by giving chilling treatments.

Stress physiology: Study of processes and function of plants in response to the stress conditions is called as stress physiology.

Stress: Any environmental condition that is capable of causing a biologically injurious change. Any environmental condition deviating from the normal situation and if that deviation affects the normal growth and developmental process that situation is considered as stress.

Strigolactones: Strigolactones are plant hormones that stimulate the branching and growth of symbiotic arbuscular mycorrhizal fungi, increasing the probability of contact and establishment of a symbiotic association between the plant and fungus. It also inhibit plant shoot branching, and trigger germination of parasitic plant seeds. *e.g.*, Striga from which strigolactones are carotenoid – derived and contain a labile ether bond that is easily hydrolised in the rhizospere, that is a large concentration gradient between areas near the root and those further away.

Stroma: Stroma is the hydrophilic matrix that is filled in the internal chloroplasts in which is embedded grana. This is a protenicious gel layer in which RuBiSCO resides.

Strophiolate: Seed with elongate aril or strophiole in the hilum region.

Strophiole: Outgrowth of the hilum region which restricts water movement into and out of some seeds. In some hard-coated legume seeds, *e.g.*, *Melilotus alba* and *Trigonella arabica*, a plug covering a special opening the strophiolar cleft must be loosened or removed before water can enter, and then only through this region.

Strophism: Torsion induced by an external factor.

Subjective day: Under constant conditions (*e.g.*, LL or DD), it is the span corresponding to the light span of a previously used 24 h *LD* environmental cycle.

Subjective night: Under constant conditions (*e.g.*, LL or DD), it is the span corresponding to the dark span of a previously used 24 h *LD* environmental cycle.

Subsidiary cells: Subsidiary cells are the special epidermal cells, which surround the guard cells of the stomatal apparatus. These cells are achlorophyllous.

Substrate level phosphorylation: Substrate-level phosphorylation is a type of metabolic reaction that results in the formation of adenosine triphosphate (ATP) or guanosine triphosphate (GTP) by the direct transfer and donation of a phosphoryl group to adenosine diphosphate (ADP) or guanosine diphosphate (GDP) from a phosphorylated reactive during the conversion of substrate into product.

Substrate: The media comprising the root environment specified as to type, amendments, and its dimensions (container size).

Subtraction library: A library of cDNAs containing only those transcripts expressed under a defined condition after elimination of transcripts from differing conditions.

Succulence: A morphological condition denoting thick, fleshy plant organs with a high water content.

Succulents: Plants having thick leaves with a high tissue-water content. Typically xerophytes that have a thick cuticle, low transpiration rates, and the high water use efficiency (WUE) associated with CAM metabolism.

Sucrose (Cane sugar): A disaccharide, non-reducing sugar made up of glucose and fructose joined together by a (1-2) glycosidic linkage.

Sulfate salinity: Salinity in which sulfate is the major anion.

Summer dormancy: Dormancy of buds established during long days of summer or early autumn, usually in preparation for winter conditions.

Sunscald: A winter injury phenomenon in which an otherwise hardy woody plant is partially thawed on its sunward side; when the sun disappears, the thawed tissues experience rapid intracellular freezing leading to injury and death.

Supercooling: Also called undercooling or subcooling. Cooling of a substance (i.e., water) below the temperature at which a change of state (i.e., liquid to ice) would ordinarily take place without such a change of state occurring. Cooling of water below its freezing point without freezing taking place; this results in a metastable state.

Suppression: The phenotypic correction of a mutation without changing any gene sequences.

Surface tension: The tension of the surface film of a liquid caused by the attraction of the particles in the surface layer by the bulk of the liquid, which tends to minimize surface area.

Susception: Sometimes the term perception is restricted to those processes that involve living structures. In this case, the very first, pure physical effect of the stimulus is called susception; e.g., displacement (sedimentation) of a statolith-like structure, or excitation of a pigment molecule.

Suspension: In chemistry, a suspension is a heterogeneous mixture containing solid particles that are sufficiently large for sedimentation. Usually they must be larger than one micrometer. A suspension is a heterogeneous mixture in which the solute particles do not dissolve but get suspended throughout the bulk of the medium.

Svedburg unit (S): It is called as sedimentation constant (S); $1\ S = 10^{-13}$s. It denotes the rate of migration of macromolecules in solution under centrifugation and is related to the molecular size and shape.

Symbiotic nitrogen fixation: It occurs in a plant that harbors nitrogen fixing bacteria within their tissue.

Symplast: The interconnected, through plasmodesmata, protoplast of the plant. Some authors would exclude the central vacuole. In a cell the living part of a plant. The symplast of a plant is the inner side of the plasma membrane of the cell in which water and low-molecular-weight solutes can freely diffuse.

Symplastic growth: Adjacent cell walls do not alter their position relative to each other, and no new areas of contact are formed; this leads to expansion with minimum shear in the cross section.

Symplastic pathway: The water first enters the cell sap and then passes from one cell to another. Such type of movement where living protoplasm involved is called symplast. It consists of living parts of plant body, *i.e.*, protoplasts connected by plasmodesmata.

Symptoms of injury: Visible manifestations of the secondary events that reflect injury to the cells and tissues caused by chilling.

Symport: Refer Cotransport.

Synthase: An enzyme which catalyses the linking together of two molecules, especially without the direct involvement of ATP.

Synthetase: Any ligases that synthesis biological compounds using ATP as a source of energy.

Synchronizer: An environmental signal that can rephase (or entrain) a rhythm. Also called the Zeitgeber. Synchronizer may be preferred since it does not convey the impression of "giving the time" (as Zeitgeber does), but merely to set the phase and/or period of an endogenous rhythm.

Systemic acquired resistance: Refer SAR.

Systemin: A polypeptide phytohormone signaling a defense mechanism in plants when it is wounded by herbivores.

T

Tannins: Group of plant phenolic compounds found in higher plants as secondary metabolites. Their main function is to defense against microorganisms, insects, and herbivores and in allelopathy.

Taxis (tactic orientation; formerly topotaxis): Movement of motile organisms, cells or organelles, the prevailing direction of which is determined by the direction of the stimulus.

TATA box (Hogness box): A sequence of nucleotides which serves as the main recognition site for the attachment of RNA polymerase in the promoter region of eukaryotic genes. Located at around 25 nucleotides upstream of the transcriptional start site. It consists of seven base consensus sequence, TATAAAA.

TCA cycle: Tricarboxylic acid cycle. It is also called as citric acid cycle or Krebs cycle, It is a step in aerobic degradation of glucose to convert into energy. During this cycle several intermediates are produced, which leads to several metabolic pathways. During this cycle, there is production of reductancts such as NADH, FADH and GTP.

Telomere: Sequences at both termini of each eukaryotic chromosome that facilitate replication.

Temperate climates: Temperate climates are those without extremes of temperature and precipitation. The changes between summer and winter are invigorating without being frustratingly extreme.

Temperature signals: Temperature signals contribute to the timing of photoperiodic growth cessation and bud set. Temperature effect plays a major role in vernalization and flowering response.

Temperature, dewpoint (T_d, °C): The temperature of an air mass at which the condensation of water vapor begins as the temperature of the air mass is reduced. Also, the temperature corresponding to saturation vapor pressure (100 % relative humidity) for a given air mass at constant pressure.

Temperature, dry bulb (T, °C): The temperature of a gas or mixture of gases indicated by an accurate thermometer protected from or corrected for radiation effects.

Temperature, wet-bulb (T_w, °C): Wet-bulb temperature is the temperature indicated by a wet-bulb sensor of a psychrometer constructed and used according to instructions.

Temperature: The thermal state of matter with reference to its tendency to transfer heat. A measure of the mean molelcular kinetic energy of that matter.

Temperature-sensitive mutation: One in which a wild-type phenotype is expressed at the permissive temperature and a mutant phenotype at a non-permissive (usually higher) temperature.

Template: The strand of DNA or RNA that serves as the model for its own replication or transcription.

Tensile strength: The ability of the substance to resist pulling without breaking. Measured as force per unit area. Water molecules have high tensile strength due to high cohesive force between water molecules. Because of this tensile strength, water moves to the top of plant without any breaking.

Tension: Negative hydrostatic pressure.

Testa (seed coat): Outer protective layer of the seed, developed from the integuments of the ovule, diploid maternal tissue.

Termination codons: Refer Non sense codon.

Tetracyclins: Antibiotics that inhibit protein synthesis in bacteria by blocking the site on ribosome so that binding of aminoacyl-t RNAs is inhibited.

Tetrazolium salt: Salt used in testing the seed viability. In oxidized state, it is soluble and colourless, but on reduction it forms red coloured triphenyl formazan.

Thawing: The process of melting of ice formed within or surrounding the organism. Ice formed within the organism may be extracellular or intracellular in nature.

Thermoavoidance: An organism that escapes high temperature (*e.g.*, by transpiration and cooling of leaves, movement of leaves in response to high temperature).

Thermo-dormancy: Thermo dormancy refers to seed sensitivity to heat or cold. Some seeds including cocklebur and amaranth germinate only at high temperatures (30°C or 86°F). Many plants that have seeds that germinate in early to mid-summer have thermo dormancy and germinate only when the soil temperature is warm.

Thermodynamics: The science that deals with flow of heat and other forms of energy into or out of a system.

Thermogenic respiration: Refer Alternate respiration.

Thermoperiodism: Growth, development, or behavioral responses of organisms to alternating day and night temperatures. In earlier research on storage of bulbs, this term referred to the requirement for different temperatures applied during different developmental stages.

Thermophile: An organism that thrives at high temperature.

Thermophilic: Having the ability to survive or even thrive at temperatures above those considered to be lethal for most organisms.

Thermophily: The tolerance of certain organisms to temperatures between 30 °C and 100 °C.

Thermostability: The ability of proteins, enzymes, membranes, etc. to maintain their integrity with increasing temperature.

Thermotolerance: The ability of an organism or its cells or other parts (tissues and organs) to survive the full impact of a temperature stress (*i.e.*, see freeze tolerance).

Thigmonasty or seismonasty: It is the nastic response of a plant to touch or vibration. Thigmonasty is different from thigmotropism since nastic movement is independent of the direction of the stimulus.

Thigmotropism: Thigmotropism is a directional growth movement of curvature which occurs in response to stimulus of contact. Thigmotropism is a movement in which a plant moves or grows in response to touch or contact stimuli. The prefix Thigmo comes from the greek for "Touch". Thigmotropism is found in twiners and tendrils.

Thioester: An ester of a carboxylic acid with thiol or mercaptan.

Thylakoids: Component of chloroplast. Present in stroma as cisternae like internal membranes.

Thymine: A pyrimidine base found in DNA.

TIBA (Triiodo benzoic acid)**:** An inhibitor of polar auxin transport.

Ti plasmid: Plasmid of *Agrobacterium tumefaciens* that confers pathogenicity in crown-gall infection.

Tissue culture: Growing of plants in aseptic conditions from isolated plant cells in solid or liquid media.

T_{max}: Temperature at which 100 % of the plants are killed.

T_{min}: The minimum temperature that results in injury.

Tolerance: Ability of an organism or its cells or other parts to survive the full impact of a stress.

Tonic effect: Change in sensitivity or responsivity to a stimulus caused by external or internal conditions.

Tonoplast: Outer membrane of vacoule.

Torsion Growth: Movement involving twisting of the organ.

Total dry matter (TDM): It is the biomass accumulated by the whole plant over a period of interval of time.

Total dry matter production (TDMP) and its distribution: The TDMP is the biomass accumulated by the whole plant over a period of time and its distribution (allocation) to different parts of the plant such as roots, stems, leaves and the economic parts which controls the sink potential.

Totipotency: The ability of a living cell to develop into a plant is called totipotency.

Toxic zone: As the nutrient concentration of the tissue increases beyond the adequate zone, growth or yield declines because of toxicity of that particular nutrient. This range of nutrient is known as toxic zone for that nutrient.

Trace elements (micronutrients): Essential mineral elements required by the plant in very little concentration (<100 mg/kg of dry matter) for their normal growth and development.

Tracer elements: Radioactive or heavy (stable) isotopes of some elements which are used to trace out some metabolic pathway.

Transamination: It involves transfer of amino group from an amino acid to the keto group of keto acid. The enzyme transaminase catalyses the reactions.

Transcript: An RNA that is copied (transcribed) from a gene.

Transcription: Generation of an RNA copy of a DNA sequence.

Transcription factor: Any group of proteins that can regulate gene activity by increasing or decreasing the binding of RNA polymerase to the DNA molecule during the process of transcription.

Transcriptome: The complete set of RNA transcripts produced by the genome at specific circumstances or by specific cell.

Transcriptomics: Study of transcriptomes.

Transferases: Enzymes involving in transfer of one group from a compound to another molecule.

Transfer RNA: Low molecular weight RNA molecules that pick up specific amino acids from cytoplasm by their 3' ends and transfer them to the template for protein synthesis on ribosomes.

Transgenic: An organism expressing some foreign genes which have been incorporated in its genome through recombinant DNA techniques.

Transduction (stimulus transduction, signal transduction, transduction chain)**:** Biochemical or biophysical events that follow perception, finally resulting in the response; transduction usually includes amplification processes and a time lag between perception and response.

Transduction: Introduction of foreign DNA into a genome by a phage vector.

Transformation: The introduction of a gene previously not inherent in the genome of an organism.

Transient cycle: Cycle of an abnormal length occurring immediately after a phase shift (or stimulus) for synchronization to a new cycle. More than one transient cycle may be observed before the usual period is re-established.

Transient gene expression: Expression of a foreign or ectopic gene that has not been integrated into a genome.

Transit peptide: The N-terminus of a protein that is recognized post-translationally and (usually) removed during transport of a protein across a membrane; see signal peptide.

Translation: Formation of a protein on a ribosome according to the instructions in an mRNA.

Translocatable hardiness promoter(s): Same as hardiness promoter(s). Substance(s) produced in response to a short photoperiod that is perceived by phytochrome in leaves and translocated in the phloem to other plant parts.

Translocation profile: A plot of solute concentration versus distance (spatial profile) or solute concentration at a particular location versus time (temporal profile).

Translocation speed (velocity): Linear distance traveled per unit time by the solution in a file of sieve elements or by a concentration front in a phloem bundle. (m/s).

Translocation: Translocation in plants means movement of water, ions and sugars form one part of plant to another part of plant.

Transon: Exons encoded separately from one another, with other genes between them or on opposite strands.

Transphosphorylation: Transphosphorylation is a chemical reaction in which a phosphate group or a phosphono group is transferred between a substrate and a receptor.

Transpiration Pull Theory: Given by Dixon and Jolly (1894) for the ascent of sap in plants. According to this theory, water forms a continuous column from root to leaf through xylem ducts because of its high cohesive and adhesive force and also because of the water potential gradient created by transpiration.

Transpiration rate: The amount of H_2O transpired by plant per unit leaf area and per unit time expressed as mmoles/m^2/s.

Transpiration ratio: It is the ratio of water transpired to the biomass produced by the plant. It is the inverse of water use efficiency.

Transpiration: Transpiration is the loss of water in form of water vapour from the aerial portion of plants. It occurs chiefly from the leaves while their stomata are open for the passage of carbon-di-oxide and oxygen during photosynthesis.

Transporters: Proteins present in the membrane which helps in the transport of specific substances.

Trans-Zeatin: Most abundant and widely distributed natural cytokinin in higher plants.

Transposition: The insertion or excision of a transposon to or from a genome.

Transposon: A transposable element or transposon is a DNA sequence that can change its position within a genome, sometimes creating or reversing mutations and altering the cell's genome size. Transposition often results in duplication of the transposable element. A transposable element usually flanked by inverted repeat sequences.

Traumatropism: The ability of growing plant organs to modify orientation as a result of injury. Unilateral injury to the tip of root produces negative traumotropism, that is ,bending of the root opposite to the injured side. Unilateral injury to the shoot apex produces positive traumotropism that is bending in the region of the injury.

T-region of Ti plasmid: The portion of a Ti plasmid that is transferred into the host genome.

Triacylglycerols: Esters of glycerol and three long chain fatty acids. It is also called as neutral fats.

Tropic Movements: The growth movement in response to external stimuli, like light, gravitation, water and touch is called as tropic movements.

Tropism: A tropism (from Greek, tropos, "a turning") is a biological phenomenon, indicating growth or turning movement of a biological organism, usually a plant, in response to an environmental stimulus.

Tumbling (tumbling phase): Irregular movement of peritrichous bacteria without locomotion, usually caused by clockwise rotation of flagella. The running phase is interrupted by a tumbling phase either autonomously in more or less regular intervals, or as a response to a phobic stimulus. Usually, the direction of movement is randomly different before and after a tumbling phase.

Turgor: Turgidity of a cell due to turgor pressure.

Turgor movement: Reversible curvature caused by asymmetric change in length or volume, either in a single cell by asymmetric elastic extension/relaxation of the cell wall upon uptake or loss of water, or in a multicellular organ by differential swelling/shrinking of cells on opposite flanks.

Turgor pressure (TP): Pressure exerted by the protoplast against the cell wall is known as turgor pressure. When a living plant cell is placed in water, it swells up due to the absorption of water by osmosis. As a result of this entry of water into the cell sap, a pressure developed in the protoplast which is exerted it against the cell wall. This actual pressure is TP and the cell wall being rigid and elastic exerts, an opposite pressure equal in magnitude to the turgor pressure. This pressure is called wall pressure.

Turgorins: A group of organic compounds that activate pulvini in leaves of *Mimosa* and *Acacia karroo* and are believed to control nastic movements.

Turnover number: Number of substrate molecules converted into product by one mole of enzyme per active site per second.

Tyndall effect: When a beam of light is passed through colloidal solution, scattering or diffraction of light by the colloidal particles takes place. This is called as Tyndall effect.

Twintron: An intron within another intron.

U

Ubiquinone (UQ): It is a lipophilic metabolite that functions in the electron transport chain in the plasma membranes of prokaryotes, and the inner mitochondrial membranes of eukaryotes, apart from its roles as an antioxidant and in the regeneration of tocopherols. Also called as Coenzyme Q.

Ubiquitin: It is a small protein that is found in almost all cellular tissues in all eukaryotic organisms,(i.e. it occurs ubiquitously) which helps to regulate the processes of other proteins in the body.

Ultracentrifuge: A high speed centrifuge with speed upto 60,000 rpm and centrifugal field of 500,000 x g

Ultradian rhythm: Biological rhythm having a period appreciably less than 24 h (usually less than 20 h). Ultradian oscillations with periods less than 30 minutes are called high frequency oscillations.

Ultraviolet (UV) radiations: Electromagnetic radiation shorter than wavelength of visible light in the region of 200-390 nm.

Uncoupler: A substance that uncouples phosphorylation of ADP by Pi from electron transport. e.g., 2,4-dinitrophenol.

Uniporter: A membrane protein either a channel or carrier protein that is involved in facilitated diffusion.

Unit membrane model: An old classical model of all biological membrane. Proposed by Robertson (1959). According to this model, the biological membrane consists of two lipid layers bounded on either side by monomolecular proteins.

Unsaturated fats: An unsaturated fat is a fat or fatty acid in which there is one or more double bond in the fatty acid chain. If they exposed to cold temperature, solidification will be lower. It is important for cold tolerance of plants as it is essential for maintaining fluidity in the membrane.

Upstream: Distal or 5’ to the promoter; opposite the direction of transcription.

Uracil: A pyrimidine base of RNA.

V

Vacuole: A fluid filled space within the cytoplasm surrounded by membrane called as tonoplast, that occupies most of the volume of cell. Aside from storage, the main role of the central vacuole is to maintain turgor pressure against the cell wall.

Valinomycin: An antibiotic that uncouples electron transport and oxidative phosphorylation only in presence of some cations such as K^+ or Na^+

Van der Waals interaction: Weak intermolecular forces between molecules as a result of each inducing polarization in the other.

Vant's Hoff equation: Equation used to find out the water potential of solution based on the concentration of solution.

Y_w = - miRT bars, Where m is molar concentration, i = ionization constant, R= gas constant and T = Room temperature.

Velamen: A special water absorbing tissue surrounding the cortex in aerial adventitious roots of many epiphytic orchids.

Vapor pressure deficit (VPD): The difference between the actual vapor pressure of water in the air and its saturated (i.e., 100 % relative humidity) vapor pressure, expressed in pascals: Pa. (Vapor density is expressed in grams of water per cubic meter of air).

Variance (S_2): The square of the standard deviation (really just an intermediate step in the calculation of the standard deviation)

Vascular bundle: A strand of conducting vessels in the stem or leaves of a plant, typically with phloem on the outside and xylem on the inside.

Vascular differentiation: The differentiation of the cambial derivations into xylem and phloem is called as vascular differentiation. It is under the control of auxins. IAA is responsible for the differentiation of cambial derivatives into xylem elements.

Vascular plants: Vascular plants are the plants which are characterized by presence of conducting tissue of xylem and phloem. Vascular plants include the clubmosses, horsetails, ferns, gymnosperms (including conifers) and angiosperms (flowering plants).

Vascular tissue: Vascular tissue is a complex conducting tissue made up of more than one type of cells. It helps in conduction of water, minerals, photosynthates etc. throughout the plant.

Vector: Plasmid; means of introducing foreign DNA into a host.

Vernalin: It is a hypothetical plant hormone. This hormone is produced on vernalization (chilling treatment) of plants and hence the name vernalin. It induces flowering in plants.

Vernalisation: Vernalisation is the artificial exposure of plants (or seeds) to low temperatures in order to induce flowering. By satisfying the cold requirement of many temperate-zone plants, flowering can be induced to occur earlier than normal in warm climates lacking the requisite cool temperature.

Viability: The state of living, growing, or developing. The viability test estimates the relative or absolute survival of an organism. For example, common cold hardiness viability tests include visual browning, conductivity, regrowth, vital stains such as 2,3,5-triphenyl tetrazolium chloride, florescein diacetate, Evan's blue, and neutral red.

Viable: Applied to the condition of a seed that is alive and capable of germination when provided with suitable environmental conditions; these conditions may include treatments to break dormancy.

Viscosity: Viscosity is the internal property of a liquid that offers resistance to flow. It is a quantity expressing the magnitude of internal friction in a fluid, as measured by the force per unit area resisting uniform flow. *e.g.*, Honey has much viscosity than water.

Visual browning: A method of determining injury to plant tissues by observing the presence or absence of oxidative phenolic browning.

Vitamins: Organic substances required in smaller amounts and having profound catalytic and regulatory functions in cell metabolism.

Vivipary: Germination of seed, when the seed is attached to mother plant i.e., precocious germination.

V_{max}: Maximum velocity of an enzyme catalyzed reaction at infinite substrate concentration.

Volume flow: Net flux of water entering sieve elements.

W

Wall pressure: The inward pressure exerted by the cell wall against expanding protoplast; equal but opposite to turgor pressure.

Warburg effect: Warburg effect states that the competition between CO_2 and O_2 for enzyme RuBisCO with CO_2 promoting photosynthesis and inhibiting glycolate formation and inhibiting photorespiration and O_2 promoting glycolate formation and inhibiting photosynthesis.

Water deficit: Water available to the plant is less than optimum requirement.

Water potential (ψ_w): Water potential is defined as free energy status of water in a system compared to the free energy status of pure water. Here system refers to water in plant cell or soil and pure water refers to the water which does not have any solute in it. Water potential is measured in terms of bars, Pascals or Megapascals and denoted by $\psi_{w.}$

Water savers: It is adopted by plants to avoid drought condition by conserving water. These genotypes save water primarily by decreasing transpiration by adopting mechanism like leaf rolling, leaf folding, waxiness on leaf surface.

Water spenders: Water spenders avoid drought by absorbing more water with traits like increased root length, increased root density, increase in root to shoot ratio.

Water status: The general condition of a plant relative to any limitations imposed by a lack of water.

Water stress: An environmental condition of either excess or lack of water, but the term is usually used to indicate a lack of water. Water stress as an environmental condition (sometimes referred to as drought stress) should be expressed as the amount of water available to a plant compared with its maximal requirements.

Water use efficiency: Agricultural WUE can be defined for a growing season either as yield per unit irrigation water applied or biomass produced per unit of transpiration, whereas instantaneous physiological WUE can be defined as moles of carbon dioxide fixed by photosynthesis per mole of water transpired. It is the ratio of amount of biomass produced to amount of water transpired. If water use efficiency is more in a genotype, then that genotype is said to have drought tolerant. Water use efficiency is more in C_4 plants.

Water vapor deficit (e_d, P_a): The difference between saturation water vapor pressure at ambient temperature and actual vapor pressure at ambient temperature.

Water vapor density (P_r, g.m-3 or P_a): The ratio of the mass of water vapor to a given volume of air, also called absolute humidity. It may also be measured as partial pressure. (Water vapor pressure).

Watering (volume, L): The addition of water to the substrate specified as to the source, the times, the amount, and the distribution method.

Watson-Crick model: Double helix (duplex) model of DNA first given by Watson, J.D. and Crick,F.H.C in 1953.

Wavelength (l): It is a fundamental unit in the study of radiant energy. The distance measured along the line of propagation between two points representing similar phases of two consecutive waves.

Western blot: Western blot is a common method to detect and analyze proteins. It is built on a technique that involves transferring of proteins separated by electrophoresis from the gel to a membrane where they can be visualized specifically.

Whiptail: Whiptail is a symptom due to the deficiency of molybdenum in cauliflower.

Wilcoxon's Signed-Rank Test: A paired comparison test where the absolute differences between pair members are ranked, then reassigned their original sign. If there is no difference between the two groups, the expected value of the sums of the signed ranks should be 0. As in many of the non-parametric tests, a special table is used to see if the difference is significant.

Wild type: The normal unmutated phenotype.

Winter annuals: Plants that germinate in late summer or autumn, spending the winter as seedlings, and flowering and fruiting during the next growing season. Flowering may be promoted by exposure to the low temperatures of winter.

Winter chilling: Temperatures adequate for the chilling requirement to break dormancy.

Wilting: Loss of turgidity of plant tissue or organs. A plant tissue or an organ becomes wilted when its turgor pressure falls to zero.

X

Xanthophylls (Carotenoids): These are tetraterpenes with general formula $C_{40}H_{56}O_2$. Xanthophylls are a class of oxygen-containing carotenoid pigments, responsible for the color of many of the yellow, orange, and red hues of flowers, fruits, vegetables (corn, pepper, etc.), egg yolks, and feathers, shells, or flesh of many animal species (flamingo, canary, shrimp, lobster, chicken, or salmonids). In plants, they are involved in photosynthesis with chlorophyll and are responsible for the red, yellow, and/or brown colors of autumn foliage as the chlorophyll levels decline.

Xeromorphy: Morphological characteristics, such as small, tough leaves, a heavy cuticle, etc., that are generally important for adaptation to dry environmental conditions.

Xerophily: The combined adaptive morphological and physiological characteristics of plants able to grow under dry environmental conditions.

Xerophyte: A plant adapted to environmental conditions of severely restricted water availability.

Xerophytes: Plants, which grow in dry habitats or xeric conditions, are called xerophytes.

X-ray crystallography: A technique to determine the three dimensional structure of a molecule by analyzing X-ray diffraction patterns produced by a crystalline compound.

Xylans: Important components of hemi-celluloses in plant cell walls.

Xylem: Xylem is the vascular tissue responsible for the transport of water and nutrients from the soil through roots to the above-ground parts of plant. It has only unidirectional movement.

Xylem loading: Transfer of water and mineral salts from symplast to conducting cells of xylem.

Xylose: A simple 5 carbon sugar (Aldopentose sugar)

Xylulose: A simple 5 carbon sugar (Ketopentose sugar)

Y

Yamogenin: A triterpene plant steroid belonging to a group of sapongenins that is obtained from *Dioscorea* and is used in making oral contraceptives.

Yang cycle: A biochemical pathway of salvaging CH_3-S group from s-adenosyl methionine, an intermediate of ethylene biosynthesis from methionine and recycling it to form sulphur containing amino acid methionine again.

Yeast artificial chromosome (YAC): A construct including centromere, telomeres, an origin of replication and multiple cloning sites for the insertion of foreign DNA.

Z

Z scheme: Refer non-cyclic electron transport.

Z-DNA: A duplex DNA structure in which helical coiling of the two polynucleotide chains is left handed and phosphate backbone of the polynucleotides follows a zig-zag course.

Zeatin: Most abundant natural cytokinin present in plant.

Zeaxanthin: Blue light photoreceptor, a xanthophyll.

Zinc finger: It is a small structural protein motif, coordinated by one or two zinc ions to stabilize the fold. Zinc fingers are structurally diverse and are present among proteins that perform a broad range of functions in various cellular processes, such as replication and repair, transcription and translation, metabolism and signaling, cell proliferation and apoptosis.

Zwitter-ion: A dipolar ion with spatially separated positive and negative charges.

Zygote: Derived from Greek word which means "Joined". A zygote is eukaryotic cell formed by fertilization between two gametes. A zygote's genome is a combination of DNA in each gamete contains all the genetic information necessary to form a new individual.

Zymase: It is an enzyme complex in yeast which brings about alcoholic fermentation of grape sugar (glucose) into ethyl alcohol with release of carbondioxide.

Zymogen: Inactive precursor of an enzyme. For e.g., Trypsinogen, the precursor of the enzyme trypsin.